A Young E
My Entire Story

Written By
David M. Smith

Copyright

The "A Young Boy Named David" series is owned by Kingdom Being Consultants, LLC. No part of this publication may be reproduced, stored in a retrieval system, or transmitted in any way or by any means, either electronically, mechanically, by photocopy, recording, or any other method, without the prior authorization by the author, except as provided by US copyright law. This book is designed to provide accurate and authoritative information with regard to the subject matter covered. This information is given with the understanding that neither the author, nor Kingdom Being Consultants, LLC, is attempting to render legal or professional advice. The opinions expressed by the author are not necessarily those of Kingdom Being Consultants, LLC.

Copyright 2022 by David Smith

ISBN: **978-8-366-90994-5**

Dear Young Reader,

Thank you for your support! I hope that my story helps you to deal with any pain that you are going through.

My goal is to help you to realize that you deserve to be happy. That is why I have written this special book...just for you! I have poured out my heart into these words.

You can also help yourself to feel better. Reading this book is the first step. Make sure that you share this book with any friend that you think might need to read it, too.

This book is based on things that really happened to me. Please know that if you ever need help, you should go to a mature adult and let them know what's going on. Also, you've always got a friend in me!

Your Friend in Life, David M. Smith

Dedication

I dedicate this book to God, my family, and any young boy or girl out there who needs to feel loved. We all have a story. Don't be afraid to share yours.

***

Feel free to invite David M. Smith for speaking, teaching, class appearances, conference keynotes, book studies, book signings, and workshops: www.d-m-smith.org

A Young Boy Named David
Book 1
My Story Begins

Written By
David M. Smith

A Young Boy Named David Book 1: My Story Begins

Written By: David M. Smith

Characters

- David – me
- Sylvia – mom
- Malcolm – dad
- Jonathan – older brother
- Larry – younger brother
- Mary – cousin
- Leslie – nurse
- Mr. Blato – building owner

Table of Contents

Copyright   2

Dear Young Reader,   3

Dedication   4_Toc121342646

A Young Boy Named David Book 1: My Story Begins   6

   Characters   7

   Chapter 1: My Story Begins   16

   Chapter 2: Meeting Larry   23

   Chapter 3: Learning About My Father   29

   Next Time…   34

   Questions to Discuss   35

A Young Boy Named David Book 2: Crazy Things Happening to Us   38

   Characters   39

   Chapter 1: The Numbers Following Us   41

   Chapter 2: The Time I Almost Drowned!   46

   Chapter 3: What Happened to Mr. Sea-Dog?! 53

   Next Time…   59

   Questions to Discuss   60

A Young Boy Named David Book 3: Running Around the House   63

   Characters   64

   Chapter 1: Lots of People Running Around   66

Chapter 2: Ballerina Running by the Steps 74
Chapter 3: Running From Miss Precious 81
Next Time... 869
Questions to Discuss 870

A Young Boy Named David Book 4: The Baltimore Blues 91
Characters 92
Chapter 1: Living on Welfare 94
Chapter 2: Baltimore Blues 99
Chapter 3: Hoping For Change 105
Next Time... 109
Questions to Discuss 110

A Young Boy Named David Book 5: My School Days 89
Chapter 1: Mrs. Salem 91
Chapter 2: Ms. Drake and Ms. Turner 97
Chapter 3: Mr. Owens 100
Next Time... 103
Questions to Discuss 104
105

A Young Boy Named David Book 6: Stealing From Mr. Denis and Other Events 136
Characters 107
Chapter 1: Mr. Denis 108
Chapter 2: Miss Virginia 113
Chapter 3: The Humphreys 117

Next Time... 121
Questions to Discuss 122

A Young Boy Named David Book 7: Young and Tough 124
Characters 125
Chapter 1: Where My Fighting Started 126
Chapter 2: A Boy Named James 131
Chapter 3: The Other James 173
Next Time... 177

A Young Boy Named David Book 8: You Can't Win Them All! 141
Characters 142
Chapter 1: A Tie in the Bathroom 143
Chapter 2: Almost Thrown Out of the Third Floor Window! 147
Chapter 3: My One Lost Fight 151
Next Time... 155
Questions to Discuss 156

A Young Boy Named David Book 9: Looking For Family 158
Characters 202
Chapter 1: Brief Memory of My Grandmother 204
Chapter 2: The Nuns Across the Street 209
Chapter 3: Where is My Father? 167
Next Time... 218

Questions to Discuss — 172

A Young Boy Named David Book 10: The Good, the Bad, and the Karate — 174

- Characters — 175
- Chapter 1: Mr. Teddy — 176
- Chapter 2: Mr. German Shepherd — 180
- Chapter 3: Mr. Conway, the "Karate Kid" — 185
- Next Time… — 188
- Questions to Discuss — 189

A Young Boy Named David Book 11: Making New Friends — 191

- Characters — 192
- Chapter 1: Jonathan, Come Back! — 193
- Chapter 2: The Humphreys — 196
- Chapter 3: Little Frederick — 200
- Next Time… — 204
- Questions to Discuss — 205

A Young Boy Named David Book 12: Angry Kids! — 207

- Chapter 1: Trying to Fight the Teacher! — 209
- Chapter 2: Anthony the Boxer — 213
- Chapter 3: The "Dark Day" — 216
- Next Time… — 220
- Questions to Discuss — 221

A Young Boy Named David Book 13:Looking Out for Mom
                                                   223

   Characters   224

   Chapter 1: Mr. Hawalfa   225

   Chapter 2: Mr. Charlie   228

   Chapter 3: Mr. Willie   232

   Next Time...   235

   Questions to Discuss   236

A Young Boy Named David Book 14: Familiar Faces   238

   Characters   239

   Chapter 1: What Was Happening to Jonathan?   240

   Chapter 2: Mr. Sea-Dog's Good Times   244

   Chapter 3: Mr. Sea-Dog's Bad Times   247

   Next Time...   251

   Questions to Discuss   252

A Young Boy Named David Book 15: Going to the Dark Side
                                                   254

   Characters   255

   Chapter 1: "Micey"   256

   Chapter 2: Stealing Purses With Willis   260

   Chapter 3: Running From the Cops!   265

   Next Time...   269

   Questions to Discuss   270

A Young Boy Named David Book 16: More School Problems
                                                                272
   Characters   273
   Chapter 1: Lessons From the Street   274
   Chapter 2: Rematch With James Johnson   277
   Chapter 3: Battle with Fang Face   280
   Next Time…   284
   Questions to Discuss   285

A Young Boy Named David Book 17: Fifth Grade Fights 287
   Characters   288
   Chapter 1: Gary vs. Gary   289
   Chapter 2: Timothy vs. David   293
   Chapter 3: Mike vs. James   297
   Next Time…   300
   Questions to Discuss   301

A Young Boy Named David Book 18: New People Moved In
                                                                303
   Characters   304
   Chapter 1: Mr. Jessie & Miss Iris   305
   Chapter 2: Miss Beatty   308
   Chapter 3: A Man Named Muscles   311
   Next Time…   315
   Questions to Discuss   316

A Young Boy Named David Book 19: Graduating to Middle School   318

    Characters   319

    Chapter 1: Sixth Grade   320

    Chapter 2: Leaving Mosher Street?   324

    Chapter 3: Seventh Grade   328

    Next Time...   331

    Questions to Discuss   332

A Young Boy Named David Book 20: Stop Right There!   334

    Characters   335

    Chapter 1: Following After Willis   336

    Chapter 2: The Grey Church   339

    Chapter 3: Blame the Person, Not the Place 346

    Next Time...   350

    Questions to Discuss   351

A Young Boy Named David Book 21: A Mother to Love Me   354

    Characters   355

    Chapter 1: More of My Mom's Family   356

    Chapter 2: Introduction to My Father   359

    Chapter 3: Mattie, My First Love   364

    Questions to Discuss   369

A Young Boy Named David Book 22: Nightmares From a New Neighborhood   371

Characters 372
Chapter 1: No Male Guidance 373
Chapter 2: Crimes With the New Kids 378
Chapter 3: A Moment I Won't Forget 383
Questions to Discuss 389

Chapter 1: My Story Begins

Hey there! My name is David. Thanks for taking the time to listen to my story. It all began back when I was born on a Wednesday, October 13th, 1969, at 8:46 pm in a hospital in Baltimore, Maryland. It was a cold place to live, but it was where I called home. I had four other brothers, which I'll tell you about later. I still remember our old address: 1720 Eutaw Place. It was an apartment building. My family lived on the basement floor.

"Come on, David. Stop staring at the gate and come inside!" my mom said. "I can't help it, mom! It's sooo tall! How high do you think it is?" I responded. For some reason, I couldn't take a single step without knowing the answer. "My guess is 50 billion feet!" my youngest brother Larry said. He was so small, that everything looked enormous. He also had a wild imagination. I knew that wasn't right, so I asked my older brother Jonathan. "Definitely not 50 billion! I'd probably say it's about six feet tall," he said. I believed him. Jonathan was smart, and I really looked up to him. "I don't care if it's 50 billion feet or six feet," my mom replied. "You boys better get both feet past that gate and go a little ways back into the cut before you get cut!"

"A little ways back into the cut" is what we called going down the narrow steps that led to our place. And "getting cut" is what my mom called spankings; she didn't actually cut us! She was tough on us, but she had to be. She was raising us all by herself. She was stressed out all the time, and us goofball boys didn't make her job any easier. Still, we knew that she loved us, and we loved her too.

Aside from Jonathan and Larry, I had two other brothers, but I never got to meet them. Sadly, they died before I was born; one died at birth and the other was a victim of his evil dad. Hey, I never said my story was a happy one. But the lessons I learned along the way helped me become the man I am today, so I still want to tell it to you.

Speaking of bad fathers, mine wasn't so great either. He abandoned my mom after having me, which is why she gave me her last name, and not his. My dad's name is Malcolm "Mack" J. King, and my mom's name is Sylvia O. Smith. "Mom, how old were you when you and dad met?" I asked one day. "Why do you want to know that? Oh, well. I don't like reliving the past, but I was twenty-one and Malc…er, your dad was twenty-seven when we had you." "What if kids think I'm weird for having my mom's last name?" "You tell anyone who gives you any problems about that to mind their own business. I just didn't want to

18

have to be reminded of your father every time I saw your name." Thankfully, I never had to worry about being made fun of for my name.

In fact, I was given a cool nickname by Mr. Blato, the owner of the building on Madison Avenue. We moved there after staying at Eutaw Place for a few years. Anyways, he always called me "Monster Mash," and eventually everyone else did, too. Why that name? There was some popular song in the 70's with the same name, and that's where he got it from. What made him link me to that song? Only he can answer that question!

Chapter 2: Meeting Larry

"No! That's my baby! I won't let you take him away from me!" My mom was hysterical in the hospital room after Larry was born. "Ma'am," one of the nurses said. I think her name was Leslie. "You clearly are in no condition to raise another child. In fact, we are prepared to call childcare services." My mother just had too many issues in her life at that time, and she could barely take care of me and Jonathan. I was only two at the time, so I don't remember every detail; I just remember that getting by every day was a real struggle for us, and my mom seemed to be totally lost as to how to make things better. Thankfully, our older cousin Mary was in the hospital room to try and talk some sense into my mother, since she was refusing to listen to Nurse Leslie.

"Sylvia, you have to listen to me. I know you want this child, but think of your situation. You barely make enough money as it is, and you know what problems you have." "Mary, I can't just put him into the system! Who will care for him like I would? How will I know that he'll be safe?" Mary thought for a second, then gave an answer that would cause me to not live with my younger brother for the first few years of my life. "I'll take him." "What?" my mom exclaimed.

"Just hear me out. You know me and my husband have been trying to have our own child for a while now. This makes perfect sense! You know he'll be safe with us." When I learned that my mom agreed to this, I was mad at her for a while. "How could you give away my brother like that? I was looking forward to being an older brother," I would say. But I didn't see the bigger picture. I only knew that I didn't get to meet Larry until I was older.

After the hospital incident, cousin Mary was given full custody of Larry. Eventually, they started coming over to visit us, and these visits became regular. Larry did well while living with them, and I have fond memories of him. "Hey Monster Mash! Let's go up to the third floor and pretend that we're astronauts!" As I said earlier, Larry's imagination was out of this world! I think he spent a lot of time in his head, trying to escape what was happening in his own body. You see, Larry had Leukemia, a bad disease that makes you really sick. "Ok Larry, but this time I get to land on the moon first!" We would always play different games when he came over. We were best friends.

Cousin Mary always dressed Larry in the best clothes. "Look at me, Monster Mash! I'm the Prince of Baltimore!" he would say when he walked through the door. "Yeah, yeah. There's no way I'm going to treat you like a prince, shorty!" Larry hated being called short. I guess in his head, he was seven feet tall, and calling him short snapped him back to reality. "Well, if I'm so short, how come I have to eat pills that are so big?" "What do you mean?" I wondered. That's when I got to see the crazy huge pills that Larry had to take every day since he was sick. I didn't think something so big could fit into his tiny mouth. I never called him shorty after that day. I had a newfound respect and understanding of what Larry was going through.

The made-up games and his dream of being tall was his own way of fighting his disease, and I didn't want to take that away from him. "Right this way, Your Highness. I have everything prepared for your arrival. Try not to hit your head on the door post." After saying that, I'd never seen Larry smile so big. I looked forward to each of his visits. Then one day, the news we were dreading finally came…I wouldn't be seeing Larry anymore.

It was a weird feeling, and hard for me to accept. He was buried in his finest clothes, like the prince that he was. He had on a light green dress shirt, a beige-colored sweater, beige corduroy pants, and some brown hush puppies. He was only five years old when we lost him. Shortly afterwards, we left Madison Avenue and moved to Mosher Street, where Mr. Blato had bought some new apartment buildings. The change of scenery was something I needed to help get my mind off things.

Chapter 3: Learning About My Father

"Hey, mom?" I said one day. "Yes, David baby?" she replied. "I think I'm ready now." "Ready for what?" she said with a puzzled look on her face. "I think I'm ready to hear more about my dad." I was almost afraid to ask her this. I knew she didn't like talking about him. But I thought that if I knew more about him, I'd know more about me. She looked away for a few moments, and I could hear her take a deep breath and sigh. "You're right. You should know about him. Just don't expect me to tell you anything good."

"Ok mom. So, where was he from?" "Your daddy, Malcolm King, lived in Halifax, North Carolina before he came to Baltimore. He has seven other siblings, and some of them are also in Baltimore." "So he came here to be around them?" I asked. "Not exactly. You see, he had gotten into some…trouble with another girl, and she was going to have a baby. Her daddy wasn't too happy with that, so he gave Malcolm two options: marry the girl, or get shot. Your daddy picked option three and ran away, and that's how he ended up in Baltimore."

"Wow. Is there anyone my dad didn't run away from?" I was beginning to notice a bad pattern with him. "No, David. I'm convinced that man would run away from himself if he could. Hey, with all the mess he gets himself into, maybe that's what he's trying to do." "Mom? Don't get mad at me for asking this…but if dad is so bad, why did you ever like him?" She just lowered her head, paused for a moment, then actually let out a chuckle. "David, I want to know the same thing. Honestly, looking back, I liked the things he said, not really him as a person. He was funny and definitely a smooth talker. And I wasn't the only one who fell for his charms." I studied my mom's face to see if she wanted to continue. I could tell that she was having memories come back to her that she didn't like.

"Mom, I don't think you are bad just because you met dad. You're different than him, and I'm glad I'm with you." She looked at me, and I could tell she had something else to say. "David, your dad never stayed in one place for too long. He met lots of women, and he got into trouble with all of them. One time, when Jonathan was a baby, I was out doing errands and stopped somewhere to use the restroom. Another woman came in and sat her baby next to mine. We both were shocked because the babies looked exactly alike. I'm certain that baby was your dad's too."

"Does that mean that was my…brother?" "Yes, David. Well, half-brother. And the baby that was born in North Carolina was your half-sister. In fact, who knows how many brothers and sisters you have running around in Baltimore, and Lord only knows where else."

I thought about all those kids, living their lives without their father, like I was. Wondering why he left them, if they did anything wrong, if they were bad. If that is your story, please know that it's never your fault when a parent leaves. You are pure and innocent, and you don't have to end up like them. "Thanks for telling me all this, mom. I promise that when I grow up, I'm never gonna be like him." Now the tears were streaming down her cheeks. She pulled me close and whispered softly, "I know, my little Monster Mash. I know."

Next Time…

Wow, it was really nice talking to you! You're a great listener. I have more stories to tell, but I'm all out of time for today. I hope you'll come back to hear more. And remember: Everyone has a story. Don't be afraid to tell yours! Next time, I'll tell you about some crazy adventures I had when we moved to Mosher Street.

Questions to Discuss

1. Why did David's mom give him her last name?

2. Why did Larry have to go stay with cousin Mary?

3. How did David feel about Larry leaving?

4. What was the effect of David's dad running away from his problems?

5. If you can relate to this story, what lessons have you learned?

A Young Boy Named David
Book 2
Crazy Things Happening to Us

Written By
David M. Smith

A Young Boy Named David Book 2: Crazy Things Happening to Us

Written By: David M. Smith

Characters

David – me
Sylvia – mom
Jonathan – older brother
Larry – younger brother
Bernard – uncle
Mr. Sea-Dog – mom's boyfriend
Miss Gail – babysitter
Lifeguard

Chapter 1: The Numbers Following Us

"Hey, Jonathan?" I said to my brother one day. "What's up, David?" "I...um...I have a question, but don't think I'm weird for asking it." "You're my little brother, so I already think that! But you can still talk to me." My question wasn't anything big. It was just something that I had noticed. "Well, have you ever felt like you were being...followed?" "Yeah. I'm pretty sure that weird guy in the alley likes to follow people around, hoping that they'll drop some money." "No, Jonathan, I'm talking about *things* following you. Like, *numbers* following you." I lowered my head in embarrassment. It sounded so dumb when I actually said it out loud. But I was surprised by my brother's answer.

"Actually, yes! My number is 3. I've lost 3 brothers, and Mosher Street is our third house. What are your numbers?" Wow! It was such a good feeling to know that I had someone I could talk to who understood how I felt. I had doubted whether telling my feelings to my brother was a good idea. But it actually made me feel like I wasn't all alone in the world. So I told him what my numbers were. "I'm so glad you know what I'm going through! For me, it's 5 and 7." "Why those numbers?" Jonathan wondered. "It's because when Larry died, he was 5 and I was 7. And now, our new address is 507. You see what I mean?" "Yeah, I do." We sat in silence for a while. It wasn't normal for us to share our thoughts and feelings, but it definitely made us feel like a weight had been lifted off of our shoulders.

"So, do you think these numbers mean anything?" I wondered out loud. Like I told you the last time we met, Jonathan was really smart, and I always looked to him to answer my big questions. He knew everything. At least, that's how it seemed to me. So I was really thrown off when he looked up at me with tears in his eyes and said, "I don't know David. I don't know." Not having the answer seemed to be really bothering him. I had never seen him like this, and I had no idea what to do. So I did what I could. I went over and gave him a hug, trying to let him know that I didn't care that he was crying in front of me. It actually made me respect him even more for trusting me to see him like that.

Then I had an idea. "Hey, why don't we pick a new number? Our own number?" "How would that help?" he asked. "Well," I said. "Instead of the numbers following us, we could use them to help us feel better. Wait a minute...let me figure something out."

All this talk of numbers was reminding me that I loved math, and I had a new equation that I was trying to work out. "Monster Mash (my nickname, remember?), what are you doing over there?" my brother said. "Oh, just figuring out our new number. And I just did! It needs to be 11." "I don't see how that helps." I knew I would have to explain it to him. "You see, my nickname, Monster Mash, has 11 letters in it. Right now, you are 11 years old. And, 11 is just a 1 and a 1 next to each other, right? And 1 brother plus 1 brother equals..." "The two of us!" he said excitedly. "Cool! I love it, David. Thanks. I think this helps."

I was glad that he felt that way. But it wasn't really the numbers that did the trick. It was the two of us, sharing our pain together, and then working together to turn that pain into something new and good. You know what I learned that day, friend? That when it comes to sharing your feelings, two people are always better than one.

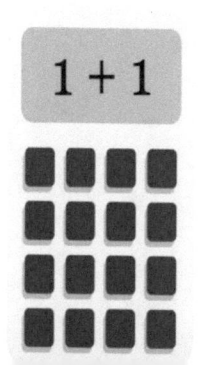

Chapter 2: The Time I Almost Drowned!

Now I want to tell you about the time when I almost drowned. Yikes! I don't even like saying that. Here's what happened. I was really young, maybe 3 or 4. I remember being with my babysitter Miss Gail at the time. "Ok David! Today you're going to learn how to swim. I'm taking you to Park Pool." That was one of the most popular pools in Baltimore back then. People would come from all over the city to swim and hang out. Adults and children would be lined up just waiting to get in. Once we finally got inside, my eyes grew wide with all the activities going on. Kids were running around, teens were jumping off diving boards that seemed to reach the sky, and the pool was jam packed with people from the shallow end all the way to the deep end.

With that many people there, you can see how easy it would be for Miss Gail to lose track of a little toddler like me. And that's exactly what happened. "Oh no! David, where are youuu? David??" To be honest, I never heard her calling my name. All I could hear was the water calling out to me. As if I was in a trance where I couldn't control anything, I found myself walking to the edge of the kiddie pool. I can't remember if my brother or anyone else from the house at 507 was there. What I'm sure of is that my mom wasn't there. In fact, growing up, there were a lot of times when my mom would leave me in the care of others. I think it had something to do with those bottles I always saw her with. They had a funny smell to them, and they seemed to make her not care about anything. She would talk funny, sleep all day, and get upset really easily.

"This…pool water…it smells funny. Could this be the weird stuff in my mom's bottles? If I get in, will I become like her? Maybe, if I did, I would understand her better and know what to do to help her." These are the thoughts that were going through my young mind. Back then, I didn't know that what my mom was drinking was alcohol, and that what was in the pool water was chlorine. Two different things that, as it turns out, could both make you drown. Drinking too much from these funny bottles was one of the problems that would later cause my mom to not be able to keep my younger brother Larry after he was born. And the funny water in the pool was about to become a problem for me right now!

Friend, let me tell you, it's really important to stay close to your parents or babysitters when you go out of the house. There are a lot of dangerous things that could happen to you, so you don't want to be all by yourself. Also, if you have anyone in your family that always drinks from those funny smelling bottles, don't feel like you need to drink it too so you can be closer to them. Stay away from that stuff! And finally, never ever walk close to the edge of the pool by yourself…*especially if you are only 3 years old, 3 feet tall, and don't know how to swim!* Alright, I've kept you waiting long enough. Here's how I almost drowned!

As I said, there were so many people at the pool that day. Even so, the lifeguard on duty, who was sitting high up in his chair, locked eyes with me. I'm so glad he did, because at that exact moment, I stepped into the pool! "Ahh! Help! He-blublub." I had fallen feet first into the water, and my cries for help became muffled as I went under. My mouth was wide open, and right away a nasty taste entered my mouth. I had never tasted water like this before!

Miss Gail heard my screams and yelled out to the lifeguard. But his chair was empty. He wasn't sitting there because he was already running full sprint to where I had fallen in. "Baby in the pool! Baby in the pool! Out of my way!" In just a few steps, he was where I was. I was splashing and waving my arms like crazy. There were so many bubbles swirling around that I couldn't see anything. Then, almost as quickly as I had fallen into the pool, I was being lifted out of it.

I had to blink and rub my face several times to get the water out of my eyes. When I could finally see again, everybody was looking at me. Too bad no one decided to notice me before I fell into the water! Well, at least the lifeguard did. After checking to make sure I was fine, he bent own and asked, "What's your name, kid?" I just stared back at him with wide eyes. I didn't know if I was in trouble or not, so I decided not to say my real name. "I'm, uh, I'm Monster Mash." He gave me a strange look at first, but he accepted it. Right before he could tell me his name, Miss Gail came running up to me shouting, "David! David, there you are!" In my little head, I was saying, "Oh no! Now he knows my real name. Thanks a lot Miss Gail!" Not knowing my thoughts, she said, "I'm so glad you're safe. Let's get you back home to your mother. Thank you so much, sir, for saving his life."

The lifeguard looked down at me and winked. "Anything for my friend Monster Mash." I never found out what happened to Miss Gail at the pool that day and how we got separated. But I do know that I'm glad there was a responsible adult, the lifeguard, was looking out for me that day. Even though I never learned his name, he taught me that there were grown-ups that could be nice and really cared about me. This was an important lesson for me to learn, because many of the adults I knew were NOT nice to me or my family. And the first man like that who pops into my mind is Mr. Sea-Dog.

Chapter 3: What Happened to Mr. Sea-Dog?!

Since my dad wasn't around, my mom had several boyfriends that would come and go. One of them was Mr. Sea-Dog, and he was not a good guy. He was very rough and violent with my mom, pushing her around and hitting her whenever he got mad. He also had a problem with the funny-smelling bottles. I didn't like him at all. But I was a little kid, and I felt like there was nothing I could do. He was older, bigger, and stronger than me and Jonathan. We were still living in Madison Avenue at the time.

"Jonathan, I don't like mom's boyfriend. He's always beating her up," I said to my brother one night. "I know how you feel, David. It's getting out of hand. But what can we do? We're just a couple of kids, and he's a grown man." "But we can't just let him keep doing this to her! We…" I paused because I thought I heard a noise outside our window. "Pssst…hey, David! Jonathan!" an older man's voice called out. We didn't recognize the voice, so we didn't respond. Then, the person outside began whistling, trying to get our attention.

Finally, he told us who he was. "Boys, it's ok. It's your Uncle Bernard. I'm your mom Sylvia's brother." I had never met anyone from my mom's side of the family. I looked to Jonathan to see if he knew that name. "Actually, yes, I do. I remember meeting him before you were born. I just haven't seen him in a long time." Even if he was our uncle, I still wasn't going to let some man I had just met come into my house in the middle of the night. Stranger danger! So we continued to talk to him through the window.

"What are you doing here so late?" I asked him. "I have a few friends who live in this building that have told me that some creep is beating up on my sister. Is it true?" Me and Jonathan looked at each other. This is what we had just been talking about! Maybe Uncle Bernard had been sent here to help us. "What you heard is true," Jonathan answered him. "What can you do about it?" We heard our uncle say a bad word under his breath. He wasn't too happy to find out that his sister was being hurt. Then he said, "Don't worry about this anymore. I'm going to take care of it tomorrow." We would soon find out what he meant by this!

The next morning, Uncle Bernard showed up to take us to our grandmother's house, where my mom and Mr. Sea-Dog were hanging out. At least it was during the day, where we could get a good look at his face. I saw his resemblance to my mother and could tell they were related. He was wearing a brown leather coat with the collar sticking straight up in the air. "Hey, Uncle Bernard? How will you take care of Mr. Sea-Dog? I don't know what that means. Are you going to talk to him?" I asked him. "Something like that," was his reply. I looked at Jonathan and shrugged. We had no idea what was about to happen. And how could we? We were just kids.

After walking for about five or six blocks, we made it to grandma's house. Once we stepped inside, Uncle Bernard went over to the bottom of the stairs and shouted, "Hey, Sea-Dog! Get down here! I've got some cold drinks, and I want to share them with you." That was weird. I didn't see Uncle Bernard bring any drinks with him. Maybe they were hidden in his coat. "Sounds nice!" Mr. Sea Dog said. "I'm not one to pass up anything free!" What happened next caught me and Jonathan off guard. As Mr. Sea-Dog came downstairs (wearing a huge smile on his face as if nothing was wrong), Uncle Bernard came from out of nowhere and bopped mom's boyfriend right in the head! Bammm! He fell down fast and hit the ground hard.

My brother and I were standing with our mouths and eyes wide open. We had never seen anything like this before! Then, Uncle Bernard stood over the man on the floor and said, "Don't you ever put your hands on my sister again! You got that?" There was no response, because Mr. Sea-Dog was knocked out! After that, Uncle Bernard took me and Jonathan by the hand and led us back home.

Uncle Bernard was our hero that day! But looking back, I realize that there *was* something me and my brother could have done before my Uncle got involved. We could have called the police. Even though we were kids, they would have listened to us and came to see what was happening with our mom. And if you think about it, hitting someone for hitting someone only makes things worse.

After that day, I never saw my uncle again. But there were plenty of other people in our new house at 507 Mosher Street that I would come to know over the years.

Next Time...

I'm so glad that we've become friends! Talking to you is so much fun. I think you're going to enjoy my next story. But remember, you can tell your story too! Trust me, doing so will help you to make sense of this crazy world. Next time we get together, I'll tell you about some of the many interesting people that I met while living at 507 Mosher Street.

Questions to Discuss

1. How did David and Jonathan feel after talking about their feelings?

2. What is your favorite number, and do you know what it means?

3. Should David have been walking next to the edge of the pool? Why or why not?

4. Was it right for Mr. Sea-Dog to be mean to David's mom?

5. Why was it a good idea that Jonathan didn't let Uncle Bernard in late at night?

A Young Boy Named David
Book 3
Running Around the House

Written By
David M. Smith

A Young Boy Named David Book 3: Running Around the House

Written By: David M. Smith

Characters

- David – me
- Sylvia – mom
- Jonathan – older brother
- Mr. Hawalfa – mom's new boyfriend
- Mr. Sea-Dog
- Miss Tree
- Miss Precious
- Miss Iris
- Mr. Denis
- Mr. Jesse
- Mr. Jenkins
- Tweety Bird
- Mr. Teddy
- The Man in the Basement

Chapter 1: Lots of People Running Around

Our house at 507 Mosher Street was the tallest building I had ever seen. To me, it looked like a big bad monster that was going to eat up me and my family. I had no idea what to expect when we moved there.

"…seven, eight, nine, ten!" "What are you counting over there, Monster Mash?" my brother said to me. "I'm counting how many steps lead up to the backdoor. There are ten giant steps!" Even more than the number of steps was the number of people living in the house. There were usually fourteen, including myself and Jonathan (the only kids living there at the time), and they were some of the strangest people you'll ever see! As for the rest of the house, it wasn't too bad. The toilet didn't always work, and it was hard to find any privacy, but I got used to it.

Now about those people we lived with! Of course, there was me, my brother Jonathan, and my mother. One day, me and Jonathan sat at the top of the steps (we lived on the third floor) and watched everyone at the house while they were running around, trying to see what they were like.

"Hey Sylvia (my mom's name), get down here! I'm ready to go out." That would be Mr. Hawalfa, my surprised!" my mom answered. Then, a scary thought popped into my young mind.

"You don't think I'll turn into a monster because my nickname is Monster Mash, do you?" "Of course you will!" Jonathan teased. He was trying to scare me on purpose. "One day you're going to go crazy and try to mash the whole place down. And then..." My mother cut him off before he could continue. "You hush up, Jonathan! Don't kid around like that. David, you don't have anything to worry about. You control who you are, not your name." That sentence stuck with me, and later on in life it came in handy!

Another drifter was Mr. Teddy. He had a family that stayed all the way in Pasadena, Maryland. Both of his kids had disabilities, which actually made them fun and interesting to hang out with! His mother would watch the kids. They had a unique view of the world around them. His son's name was Teddy Jr., and I forgot his daughter's name. Mr. Teddy didn't live at the house; he would just come to 507 around the first of the month and on the weekends. Whenever he did come by, he would stay for a few days before going back to his mother and kids.

507 Mosher Street became a place that people would come to so they could hide from their problems

and forget about life for a while. If so many people in the city were having a hard time, you would think that someone would have tried to help them! But there they were, all hanging out around my house. Because of this, I witnessed some events that a child should never have to see! Maybe that's happened to you too. All you can do is take those memories and learn from them. Use them to help make you a better person and to grow wiser. For example, this story that I'm about to tell you next taught me that you have to be careful when you're by the stairs!

Chapter 2: Ballerina Running by the Steps

I think I was in love with Miss Precious, but Miss Peaches was also very pretty. Her skin was a lovely shade of brown, and she was always really nice to me. "Hey little Monster Mash! What's new with you?" she would say to me whenever we met. However, she would have other words for my mother...words that no kid should ever say or hear! It was my mom that started it. It seemed like she had a problem with every woman at the house! "Oh, look what the cat dragged in!" she said to Miss Peaches one day. "Sylvie, don't make me come over there and pop ya one time!" Miss Peaches yelled back. I hated being in between them when they fought. I liked them both. But they sure didn't like each other!

In my mind, I thought about Miss Peaches as a ballerina. "Miss Peaches, did you ever dance when you were younger?" I asked her once. "Now what do you mean, younger? I'm still young right now!" she answered. Here's a tip for you young men reading: don't ever question a woman's age! She continued, "no, I've never danced, but I like to move real softly and carefully so people don't know that I'm coming." Even so, there came a night when Miss Peaches steps were so loud that the entire house heard it!

I mentioned earlier that Miss Peaches was always having people over. Well, what I came to find out is that when you have a bunch of adults in one room at Mosher Street, you can be sure that there will be alcohol in that room too! This is that funny liquid that comes in those brown bottles. My mom liked that stuff, but she didn't drink it nearly as much as Miss Peaches! One night she clearly had been drinking too much. She came out of her room late at night with a drink in her hand and peach fuzzy slippers on her feet. I honestly have no idea why I was even awake at that time. Maybe I couldn't sleep. But what I was about to see would give me nightmares and keep me up for years to come!

"Miss Peaches?" I whispered. "What are you doing?" I followed her down near Miss Precious' room. She looked at me, held her fingers to her lips, telling me to hush. Then, without taking her eyes off of me, she started walking forward. I smiled at her. The moon was shining on her face, and for a moment I thought she was even prettier than Miss Precious! But as she was about to pass the stairs, she all of a sudden LOST HER BALANCE! It turns out that bad liquid makes it hard for you to walk straight if you drink too much of it. So she should never have been drinking and walking so close to a dangerous area. Her light, soft footsteps were replaced with a loud BANG, BOOM, CRASH, OUCH, HELP, SLAM!!! She hit all thirty-two steps on her way down.

I was in shock at first, but then I started screaming and shouting and jumping up and down like a mad man. "Miss Peaches! Someone, help! Call 911, Miss Peaches fell down the stairs!" I don't know if it was because of my screaming or the loud banging, but everyone rushed out of their rooms to see what was going on. "David, what happened?" Mr. Teddy said. The fact that he called me by my real name shows that he knew the situation was serious. "I, she, um, it was so fast, the bottle, the fall..." I couldn't even make a complete sentence, I was so shaken up. He took one look at her body at the bottom of the steps, then immediately ran back into her room to use her phone and call for help.

The next person I saw was my mom. I didn't know how she was going to react. After all, she didn't like Miss Peaches, and they called each other names. "David? David, please tell me you're not hurt?" "Look mom," I pointed to the bottom of the stairs. "Look what happened to Miss Peaches!" It turns out that my mom was the one who called the ambulance. That really impressed me. I learned that even when you have enemies, you need to help them when they need to be helped. The ambulance got there quickly, and I watched two men get out, put Miss Peaches on a stretcher, and drive away. I never saw her again after that. My hope was that she recovered and stopped drinking from those bottles but Miss Peaches passed.

"Mom, why did you ever hate Miss Peaches in the first place?" I asked her a few days after the accident. "When your father left me, all of a sudden I didn't have anyone giving me attention. So I guess whenever I see another pretty woman getting noticed, it brings back some of those lonely thoughts. And I try to fight them away." With that honest answer, I understood my mom a lot better. I later found out from someone at the house that Miss Peaches had also been left by someone she cared about. That's why she used the bad liquid and all the people around her to try to make herself feel better. But in the end, it only led to her getting hurt even more.

My friend, when people leave you, don't drink stuff or do stuff or fight people to try to make yourself feel better. Find someone to love and be friends with. That way, what happened to the ballerina on the steps won't end up happening to you. Instead, you'll have someone you can dance with!

Chapter 3: Running From Miss Precious

"Jonathan, I wish there were some other kids in this house." "Why does it matter?" he said. "Because I'm tired of seeing adult stuff all the time! Everyone in this house does strange things, and it's starting to creep me out!" "Man, what are you talking about? What did you see that made you so upset?"

"Well," I began to tell him. "It has to do with Miss Precious." She used to be very beautiful. But her bad habits began to take all of that away. The bad liquid and some of the other things she was putting in her body was causing her hair and teeth to fall out. Not only that, but she was beginning to see and hear things that weren't really there. "Come on, tell me what happened David!" my brother said impatiently.

"Well, I was on my way outside to go to school. But when I passed Miss Precious' room the door was wide open." "Monster Mash! Get in here, I need your help!" She smiled at me, but without most of her teeth it was actually kind of scary. She was obviously in the room by herself, but she was acting as if something was watching us. "Look under the bed, Monster Mash! Do you see them?"

"Oh, wow!" Jonathan said excitedly. "Who was hiding in the room?" "That's the thing, Jonathan. There was nothing there! I even looked in her closet, but I couldn't find anything." "Well, what did she think she saw?" "Snakes!" I said. And it's true. Miss Precious actually thought that snakes had made their way into her room. I felt bad for her. The bad things she was putting in her body were ruining her life, and it was sad to see. But what happened next made me have different feelings.

"Oh, no," she then said. With a scared look on her face, she pointed a finger at my head and said, "the snakes…they're on you now!" Boy, when she said that, I ran out of that room and down the steps lightning fast! I couldn't get away fast enough.

"That is crazy, David! Who would have thought that the beautiful Miss Precious would have turned out like this?" Sad to say, but this wasn't the last time something like this would happen. Another time, she called me into her room, and this time Jonathan was with me. "Boys, get in here. I need your help!" Miss Precious cried out to us. We were nervous about going into that room again, but we did it anyway.

"What do you need?" Jonathan asked her. "Can you please talk to the two men in the yellow raincoats?" she said. "Um, Miss Precious?" I replied. "There's no one here but us!" "No, they're here!" she insisted. "They came in through the window." There were a few things wrong here. First her window was eighteen feet off the ground. Second, there was no way for someone to climb up the wall to get to her room. And third, there was no rain in sight, so why would anybody be wearing a raincoat?!

Miss Precious really thought those men were in her room, so she curled up in a ball on the floor and started crying and shouting. Jonathan and I were getting a very strange feeling, so we had to leave. At this point, there was nothing left we could do.

Despite these weird times, I still remember good things about Miss Precious. She was always sharing food. If anyone you know ever starts to say or do strange things, it might be because of how they are living their lives. There are some things you can do to your body that can really mess it up, so it's good to just stay away from all that and keep yourself clean and safe.

Next Time...

I'm glad we could meet up today! It was a fun time. Hopefully hearing about some of the things I've been through will help you deal with any problems you have in your own life. When I see you again, I want to tell you more about what my life was like back then and how it affected me and my brother. And remember, everyone has their own story. Don't be afraid to share yours!

Questions to Discuss

1. What do you think about David's new house?

2. Why should you be careful around stairs?

3. What phone number do you call when there's a serious accident?

4. What can happen if you put bad things into your body? (like Miss Precious)

5. Do you think the adults handled their problems in the right way?

A Young Boy Named David
Book 4
The Baltimore Blues

Written By
David M. Smith

A Young Boy Named David Book 4: The Baltimore Blues

Written By: David M. Smith

Characters

- David – me
- Sylvia – mom
- Jonathan – older brother
- Mr. Blato – building owner
- Mr. Hawalfa – mom's new boyfriend
- Mr. Teddy

Chapter 1: Living on Welfare

Every month, my mom would get money from the government. They sent it by mail. We needed that money to eat, pay for our room, buy clothes...we lived on it. And it always came on the first day of the month. "Did the mailman make his run yet?" she would say when she got up in the mornings at the beginning of the month. That was her way of saying, "did the mail get delivered?" Me and my brother would be waiting all day for that check to come.

"Come on, where is he?" I said. We had been sitting on the front steps for hours, but there was no mailman in sight. "Maybe this is one of the months where he isn't running," Jonathan answered. And that would happen every now and then. What we didn't know was that the months we didn't get the government check, my mom already knew ahead of time. She would have to ask other people for money, and she was embarrassed by this, so she wouldn't let us know.

It wasn't really a lot of money that we got. But we were still excited when it came. Something is better than nothing! And it was good to know that we could always go to Mr. Blato to lend us money if we were short. In fact, everybody in the house would borrow money from him. With as many times as the people in the house needed money, he must have been rich!

He was also smart. He kept track of everything. One day, he showed me a little black book that he had. "What's that, Mr. Blato?" He replied, "this is how I keep track of what people owe me. I write down how much they asked me for, and when they have to pay it back. I even have them sign it, just in case they want to "forget" that they borrowed anything." I looked through the book quickly and saw my mom's name and how much she owed that month. Let's just say that it was a really big amount!

I really wanted to help, but I couldn't think of anything I could do. That's when me and my brother had an idea that I'm not proud of. We decided to steal from people in the house. We used the money we took to give to our mom so she could pay back Mr. Blato. All we had to do was sneak the money into the envelope that she would hand him each month. We would wait until she went to sleep and sneak into the room.

Nobody and nothing in the house was safe from us. If you had money in your room, pocket, socks or closet, we'd find it. We told ourselves that it was for a good reason…but please know that stealing is never the answer. Yes, we were poor. But you can always find another way by working together and doing the right thing. The truth is, life in Baltimore back then had a lot of people doing all kinds of things just to get by.

Chapter 2: Baltimore Blues

Me and my brother were left alone a lot. Because of this, we got into a lot of trouble. Isn't it hard to make good choices when you have no one to tell you right from wrong? I could tell that Jonathan was really being affected. "Hey big brother! Want to go play in the park?" I asked. "Leave me alone! I don't want to play stupid kid games anymore! I'm gonna go steal from people outside of the house. Everyone here is too broke." This was something new. Leaving the house to steal from strangers? I didn't think that was a good idea. But what could I do to stop him? Looking back, I could have told an adult. The thing is, I used to steal too. So I thought that if I told on him, I would also get in trouble. Friend, speaking up is always the right thing to do, even if you're the one who did something bad.

Another reason why I didn't say anything was because my mom wasn't in a good place, and I didn't want to give her another thing to worry about. There was a lot going on at 507 Mosher Street at that time. My mom had moved on to her new boyfriend, Mr. Hawalfa, and he wasn't much better than Mr. Sea-Dog. He was really quick to get angry if something didn't go his way. "Mr. Teddy! Yo, Mr. Teddy!" I saw Mr. Hawalfa banging on Ms. Precious's door one day called out Mr. Teddy's name. I hid around a corner to try to listen to what was going on. "What do you want, man? It's too early for all this noise," Mr. Teddy said. "Where's my money? I need it so I can pay back Mr. Blato tomorrow," my mom's boyfriend demanded. "Oh, right. About that…I don't have it. Come see me next week." Before Mr. Hawalfa could respond, Mr. Teddy slammed the door in his face.

What happened next shocked me! Mr. Hawalfa was so upset that he *punched the plaster wall and left a hole in it!* Actually, after seeing this, I went from being shocked to scared. This was the same angry man who was around my mom all the time. How could she be safe with a man like that? On a different day, he was over at our house, and me and Jonathan could hear him and my mom arguing. We couldn't tell exactly what they were saying, but we definitely heard the last part, when Mr. Hawalfa screamed, "Do you hear me?" How could she not hear him when he was screaming at the top of his lungs? I could just see him with a huge vein popping out of his head, and his neck and spit flying out of his mouth.

"That's it. I can't just sit here and listen to this," Jonathan finally said. "But what are you…" I began to speak, but he didn't let me finish. Mr. Hawalfa was surprised to see that Jonathan actually tried to fight him back! After that, he wasn't really mean to my mom when Jonathan was around; only when I was there. I started sleeping with the door locked, trying to keep all the bad problems far away from me.

But one thing I couldn't avoid was being hungry! My mom was also getting food stamps in addition to the welfare check, but there were still times when there was little for us to eat. I once made the mistake of complaining about being hungry, and boy, do I regret doing that! "Why is there never anything good to eat in this STUPID FRIDGE!" I yelled. Out of nowhere, my mom burst into the kitchen. "David Malcolm Smith!" Uh-oh. Full name. Never a good sign! "You watch your mouth and learn to be grateful for what we have! You think I don't want us to have more? This is the best I can do right now."

I should have just said, "yes, mom," and been done with it. But I had a smart mouth back then. So instead, I said, "I'm grateful for nothing because all we have is nothing!" That set her over the edge. She chased me around the house, moving faster than I'd ever seen her move before. When she finally caught me, BAM, BAM!! She popped me so hard that I got a headache. My mom didn't usually treat me like that, but I had really hurt her feelings.

We have to remember that the parents we live with are doing their best. And even if there's not much food or clothes or toys, we need to say grace and be thankful for whatever is there. Our parents have their own thoughts and feelings that they have to deal with, plus taking care of us and going to work and whatever else they have to do. I should have been more understanding. My mom had a tough situation, and she was doing her best to take care of us while she was singing the welfare-check-not-running, money-borrowing, mean-boyfriend, Baltimore Blues.

Chapter 3: Hoping For Change

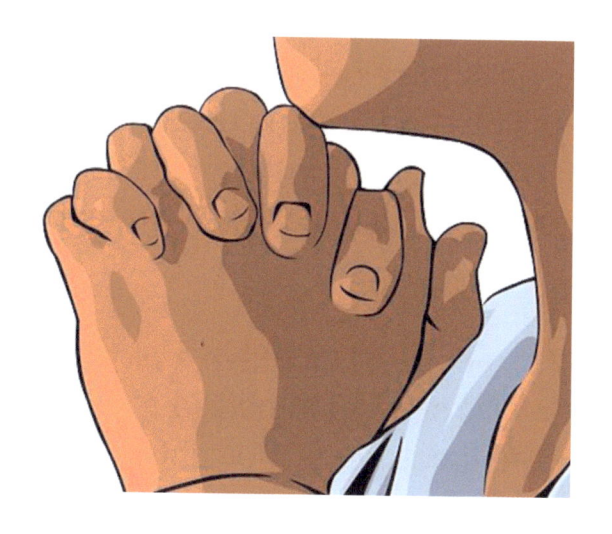

Despite all the problems in my life, there was a bright spot. The nuns across the street were the nicest people around. Not only did they give us food, but they gave me work to do that kept me busy. I felt like I was finally getting the guidance I needed. They never turned anyone away, and I felt safe whenever I was there. Too bad I couldn't live there!

At the house, I did have a bit of hope as well. Mr. Blato was starting to be like a father figure. There were times when the lights in the house would be cut off, and he would come and get me to hang out in his room. "What happened to the lights?" I asked him. "I'm tired of all the people in the house running up my bill, so I'm shutting them off." It sounded harsh to me, but I liked him paying attention to me.

Winters were rough. Because the people in the house were very wasteful, he didn't always keep oil in the house. So when it got really cold, we would all have to huddle together in the kitchen to keep warm. We would pack into there with our blankets and turn on all the oven burners. One winter, it was so cold in the house that me and my brother could see our own breath!

Eventually, for whatever reason, Mr. Blato stopped paying much attention to me. I was left to follow in my brother's footsteps. He was turning into a little thief, and I was right there with him. Without a male figure in my life, I became a product of my environment. That means the anger of Mr. Hawalfa, the pain of seeing people fall down the stairs, the struggles of being poor, and the bad influence of my brother was leading me down a violent path. I was becoming filled with anger, and my emotional problems would only get worse at school. I was hoping for a change, but it didn't seem to be anywhere in sight.

Next Time…

Being young and angry all the time is not a good combination! But I want you to know that there are better ways to deal with your pain than fighting everyone around you. You can actually look to your teachers for help and guidance if you aren't getting it at home. I'll tell you more about this next time. And remember, everyone has a story. Don't be afraid to share yours!

Questions to Discuss

1. Should you steal from others if you don't have a lot of money?

2. How do you think Mr. Hawalfa's anger issues made David's mom feel?

3. Should David have complained about not having enough food in the house?

4. How did David feel when Mr. Blato stopped paying attention to him?

5. How do you think these emotions will affect David when he goes to school?

A Young Boy Named David
Book 5
My School Days

Written By
David M. Smith

A Young Boy Named David Book 5: My School Days

Written By: David M. Smith

Characters

- David – me
- Mrs. Salem
- Loudmouth kid
- Ms. Turner
- Ms. Drake
- Mr. Owens
- Sylvia – mom

Chapter 1: Mrs. Salem

The problems I was having at home were also affecting me at Eutaw Marshburn Elementary, where I went to school. I was getting into a lot of fights and causing a whole lot of trouble. It got so bad that the school system tried to get me professional help. They wanted to know where my problems were coming from, but I already knew. Mr. Blato was the closest thing to a father I ever had, and when he stopped being close to me, I lost all hope. "If he doesn't want me, no one will!" I thought to myself. This thought made me angry, and I tried to deal with it by being a tough kid with an attitude. I said bad words and tried to beat up anyone that made me upset.

One of my few good memories of school was my first-grade teacher, Mrs. Salem. "Good morning, David!" she would say to me each morning. Normally, when people called me David instead of Monster Mash, it was because I was in trouble. But with Mrs. Salem, I could tell that she really liked me, and that gave me a special feeling. It's a good thing I liked her so much, because one day she did something to me that caused me a lot of pain!

"Wow! What is that smell?" I said before class started one day. It was a strong scent that my nose wasn't used to. Mrs. Salem smiled at me and said, "you've never smelled coffee before, have you?" "No, ma'am," I answered. It smelled REALLY good! And it must have been hot, because I saw some steam coming out of her cup, and she could only drink it in small sips.

"Alright, class," she began, getting our lesson started for the day. "Let's start by opening up our books to page five..." Before she could finish, she was cut off by the kid sitting behind me. "Mrs. Salem, I can't find my book!" The kid was practically shouting! I don't remember their name, but I just remember thinking to myself, "what a loudmouth!" "Don't worry," Mrs. Salem replied. "We have extra books in the back." With her cup of coffee in hand, she got up and made her way to get the extra book.

Now, you may have something bad happen to you, and you might be scratching your head as to why it happened at all. Whose fault was it? What did I do to deserve this? But sometimes, there's no one to blame. You could have just been in the wrong place at the wrong time. Like on that day in Mrs. Salem's class...it wasn't the kid's fault for losing their book. It wasn't Mrs. Salem's fault for bringing her coffee with her to make such a short trip to get the extra book. And it wasn't my fault for being assigned to sit where

I was. When Mrs. Salem tripped on the carpet and her arms went flying in the air, dumping all of that hot, burning coffee right on to my head, I was just in the wrong place at the wrong time. But friend, knowing that didn't take the pain away one bit!

"AAAAAAHHHHHHHHH!!!!" I had never screamed so loud in all of my life! I heard mixed reactions from the other students. Some were laughing (I guess they didn't know what it was like to be burned beyond belief), some were yelling in shock, and others were crying. Mrs. Salem sprung into action. "Oh, David, poor boy! I am so sorry! Someone get the nurse. Here David, come put your head under the sink. I'll run some cold water over your head. And everyone laughing, shut up right now! You are the ones who will clean up this mess!"

I began this story saying that I liked Mrs. Salem, right?? Well, this was one of the reasons why. I had never seen someone so concerned with the pain I was feeling. It's sad that it took a situation like this for me to figure it out, but it was nice to see someone actually show that they cared about me. Hopefully you guys can have someone show their love without hot coffee being poured all over you!

Her care for me even came through outside of school. I can remember a time when I was playing outside after dark, and I accidentally sliced my hand open. It seemed like trouble and pain followed me wherever I went! Anyways, I had to go to the hospital to get surgery, and who do you think showed up to check on me? None other than Mrs. Salem! "M-M-Mrs. Salem?" I said. I couldn't believe it. I had never seen a teacher outside of school before. "Hello, David. Your mother told me what happened. I came to make sure my little friend was alright." "You mean, we are friends?" The concept of being friends with an adult was crazy! As nice as Mr. Blato ever was to me, he never called me his friend. This was my first!

"Of course we're friends David! Here's a fruit basket I brought you. When you get better, I'd like to invite you over to have dinner with me and my husband." (As it turns out, they lived right across the street from the place where my Uncle Bernard had knocked out Mr. Sea-Dog!) After hearing her offer, I began to cry. She thought it was because I was in pain. What she didn't know was that my tears were for the emotions coming up in me that I thought I would never feel…I was crying because I finally felt loved by someone in authority.

Friend, there's an adult out there that will love you, too. They may not be in your family. They may be a counselor or a teacher or a police officer. But don't stop looking for love until you find your Mrs. Salem. Oh, and did I mention? The word "salem" means peace. May you find your true peace!

Chapter 2: Ms. Drake and Ms. Turner

Me and Mrs. Salem stayed friends the whole time I was in elementary school. When I went to third grade, I got two new teachers, Ms. Drake and Ms. Turner. They were good teachers, but they were a lot rougher than Mrs. Salem! If you got out of line, they would grab your ear and twist until it hurt! Teachers back then could do things that would not be accepted today.

I definitely got my ear pulled a few times. One time, I was being really rowdy before class started. "Ok David. Calm down before I come over there and get your ear!" I should have stopped then and there, but I kept on acting up. I was whispering loudly about how funny Miss Turner looked with her wide-frame glasses hanging off of her nose. Well, that was the final straw! She pulled my ear harder that day than she ever did before. Afterwards, Ms. Drake took me aside and told me something I had never heard before. She told me, "David, I know you can do good."

When someone puts faith in you, it gives you a strong feeling of confidence. The rest of that day, I was on my best behavior. I only wish that I had more people telling me that more often. Maybe I would have been able to avoid all the crazy fights I got into later. Just in case you've never had anyone tell you that, I'm here to let you know that you can do good too. There is good and bad inside everybody, and you always have a choice in which one you choose.

Even though they could be as mean as bulldogs sometimes, I thank Ms. Drake and Ms. Turner for being hard on me and helping me to believe in myself. It was that one-two punch combo of strict and encouraging that provided at least some positive influence on me during my school days.

Chapter 3: Mr. Owens

It turns out that even though I was a violent and angry kid, I would respond well to any adult who showed me love and affection. Principal James Owens was one of those adults in my life. He was a well-respected man, and by the time I made it to the third grade, he began to hear about a little troublemaker in his school named David Smith. And how could he not hear about me? I was getting suspended over and over, fighting kids left and right, and acting like a tough guy. Still, Mr. Owens showed a warmth to me that reached deep into my little heart.

One day, he called a meeting with me and my mom to discuss my conduct. "Miss Smith, thank you so much for meeting with me today. I'm sure by now you are aware of your son's conduct. How are things at home? Is there anything we can help you with?" "Sure," my mom answered. "You can give me some money, move us into a mansion, and keep all the bad men away from me. Oh, wait, you can't! So why don't you let me raise my own son and mind your own business!" I couldn't believe my mom was talking to my principal like that! It sounded like she was mad enough to want to fight him. But as usual, Mr. Owens just flashed his bright smile and remained calm. Looking back, he easily could have made a phone call, reported my home situation, and had me taken away from my mother. Instead, he offered help.

"Ma'am, I understand that you guys have a lot going on. The school does offer free counseling sessions. Maybe there are some prescriptions David can take to help. I can connect you to a child therapist for…" "I'm gonna stop you right there. We can't afford that nonsense, so this meeting is over." My mom didn't want to listen to a thing Mr. Owens said. But from that day forward, he gave me special attention. I could tell that he was reaching out, and I really appreciated the effort.

Always be on the lookout for people who take an interest in how you are doing. At first, you may want to shut them out. But try to let them in. They may be the only chance you have at being treated like a person who matters…don't miss out on that chance!

Next Time...

My school days definitely got off to a rocky start! I'm grateful for all the teachers who I met during my elementary days. They were a good contrast between the people I was growing up around and living with. Why don't you meet me here tomorrow, and I'll tell you about these bad influences. And don't forget that we all have a story. Be sure to share yours, too!

Questions to Discuss

1. Is it possible for everyone to be good?

2. Was it anyone's fault that the coffee was spilled on David?

3. Can teachers and students be friends?

4. What is something that you are thankful to your teacher for?

5. What should you do when trusted adults show that they really care about you?

A Young Boy Named David
Book 6
Stealing From Mr. Denis and Other Events

Written By
David M. Smith

A Young Boy Named David Book 6: Stealing From Mr. Denis and Other Events

Written By: David M. Smith

Characters

- David – me
- Jonathan – older brother
- Sylvia – mom
- Mr. Denis
- Miss Heraldine
- Miss Virginia
- Willis Humphrey

Chapter 1: Mr. Denis

I've got to tell you about my main man, Mr. Denis! He was the funniest man at the house. But not because of his jokes...we just liked to laugh at his behavior. It would really crack us up to see him running out of his room after getting robbed. He would bust out of his door in his military uniform (which he almost always wore) and shout, "who took my money?!" Most times, it was me and my brother who had done it.

Looking back, I see now that it is wrong to laugh at other people's problems. After all, one day you could be in the same position, and would you want someone laughing at you at that point? But that was a lesson I didn't know about then. So we kept stealing from him and laughing at him. Oh, and did I mention that Mr. Denis was a really short man?

"Man, look how short he is," Jonathan said to me once. "I bet I could beat him in a game of one-one-one, easy." "He may be short," I replied, "but he's still a grown man. Besides, you know he was in the army, right?" "Doesn't mean the shorty is good at basketball!" Wow! Hearing the term "shorty" reminded me of what I used to call my younger brother, Larry. Just like that, the pain was back, even if it was just for a little while.

Honestly, I believe it was the pain me and Jonathan were going through that was causing us to steal. After all, we had people and time stolen away from us, so why not steal from others to try to make up for it? Of course, doing bad things will never fill the hole in your heart left by sad events. I hope you can learn from my mistakes and not go down the road of crime.

Anyways, let's get back to my story. If you remember, the mailman would "run" on the first of each month to deliver the government checks. This was the time when me and my brother would plan to rob people. We studied people's patterns, memorized when they came and left, figured out where they hid their money, and things like that.

Mr. Denis lived in a room that had two doors you could enter. We could easily get inside both of them. It got to a point where we would fight with each other to see who would rob him first. One day, my brother came up with his own plan to beat me to the punch. Apparently, Mr. Denis was hanging out with Miss Heraldine in his room. Instead of waiting for her to leave, Jonathan used her as a distraction. He snuck into the room from the entrance that Mr. Denis had his back to. When Miss Heraldine looked over his shoulder and saw my brother crawling on his knees, she immediately knew what he was doing. That's when she decided to keep Mr. Denis distracted so my brother wouldn't get caught robbing him!

Jonathan was able to steal a big stack of money from Mr. Denis' pockets. That time it was $400!! After he snuck back out of the room, Mr. Denis realized that his pockets were empty, and he got really mad and blamed it on Miss Heraldine! Of course, she denied it and left the room. In the hallway, she met up with my brother.

"Little Jonathan! Who knew you had it in you to steal from a poor old man like that! I want half, or I'm gonna turn you in!" she said to him. "Fine! You were a good distraction. Here's $100, half of what I stole." Turns out my brother was a thief *and* a liar! Not the best role model for me. But who else did I have?

I can remember another time we stole from Mr. Denis. Or, should I say, *tried* to steal from him! We snuck into his room like normal, and he looked like he was asleep. "David, you look in his closet, while I check under his mattress," my brother whispered to me. We had never been caught before.

But this time, when my brother crept up to his bed, Mr. Denis popped up, grabbed my brother's wrist, and shouted, "caught you, brat! I knew you fools were the ones takin' my cash! I ougtha smack the dickens outta ya both!"

We ran out of there like we were The Flash! Although we were startled in his room, we went to our room and busted out laughing. It was hilarious to get threatened by such a short, angry man! This was especially true since Mr. Denis was known for yelling at people, then running in his room to hide from them! With all the dark times we were going through, stealing from Mr. Denis became something we did just for laughs and giggles! Later, an event would happen at the house that wasn't so funny.

ONLY $400

Chapter 2: Miss Virginia

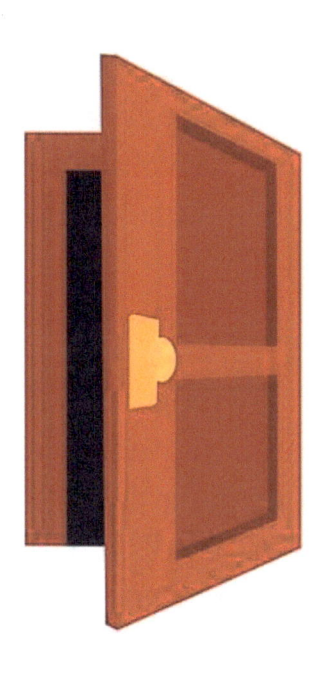

Why were people always falling around me? I can't believe how many times I was around when people had bad accidents involving the stairs. I was shocked that it happened one day to sweet Miss Virginia. Not only was she nice to me, but she was friendly with everyone in the house. "Well, hello there!" she would greet everyone, with a huge smile on her face. It was hard to be in a bad mood around Miss Virginia!

Well, unless you were my mom! She didn't like any other women hanging around the house. One time, she even tried to fight Miss Virginia! "You think you're so nice and pretty, don't you?" my mom hollered at her one day. "Maybe I'll knock some of those teeth out of your mouth!" Miss Virginia never fought back, though. She was smart enough to know that my mom was going through her own problems that were making her act crazy like this.

That's another reason why I liked Miss Virginia so much. She seemed to really understand people. She told me once, "your mom isn't fighting other people. She's fighting herself. Whatever is going on in her mind, I pray she works it out." Not many people at 507 Mosher Street prayed, but Miss

Virginia did. Too bad she didn't have more time at the house. We all could have learned a lot from her.

Here's where things went sideways...literally! She was walking past the basement door, which was always, and I mean ALWAYS, locked! And like with the other falls at the house, I just randomly happened to be there to see it all go down. Who knows why she tripped and fell to the left? Who knows why the basement door decided to swing open? I used to believe that I was cursed, that bad events followed me around wherever I went. It took me a long time to see that this wasn't true. But for a while, I was really sad and scared all of the time, waiting for the next bad thing to happen.

I hope you all know that bad things that happen around you are not your fault. Things just don't always go as planned. You were just at the wrong place at the wrong time. Like with me and Miss Virginia. I couldn't do anything but stare at her as she tried to catch herself. But instead, she tumbled down those steps and hit the wall at the bottom. I don't know if the creepy guy who lived down there was home at the time, but someone called 911 to come get Miss Virginia and take her away.

"Mom," I asked after this scary event. "What is it, David?" "I think that you need to stop fighting the women in the house. You're actually fighting yourself when you do that. I pray that you can work on yourself and get better." I could tell that she was surprised to hear me say this. After all, I was barely eight years old at the time! "What in the world are you talkin' that nonsense for, Monster Mash? Where did you get that crazy idea from?" she said to me. I looked up at her with tears in my eyes. "From Miss Virginia."

Chapter 3: The Humphreys

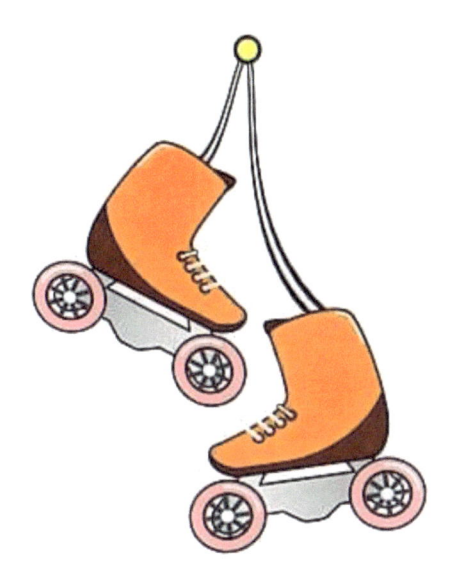

There was a new family in town, and they were no joke! Prepare to meet…the Humphreys! One of the Humphrey boys, Willis, was the scariest kid I had ever seen! He introduced me and my brother to one of our worst habits, and that was stealing. He became friends with my brother first, and it wasn't long until I was following right behind them.

"Yo, Jonathan! Wanna go roller skating with us?" Willis asked my brother. "Sure! Let me get my skates. I'll be right out." I got so jealous whenever my brother would go out and play with his new friends. "Don't you like hanging out with me anymore?" I begged with a sad voice. "Hush up, David! No one likes to have their little brother follow them around all the time. These guys are cool. Just stay here and out of our way."

This really hurt me. At this point, Jonathan was the only friend I had. Also, we didn't have many toys to play with. So when he left with our only pair of skates, what was I supposed to do? Actually, we did have one extra skate lying around. I think Willis left it behind on one of his times coming over. Even though using just one skate would be hard and looked ridiculous, I grabbed it and ran out of the house. I wasn't going to get left behind this time!

I realize now that the reason I was so set on hanging out with my brother and his friends was because it was a way for me to get out of our crazy house! When I caught up with them, I saw a bunch of kids zooming down the street, going at least 30 miles per hour. Wow! They were keeping up with some of the cars that were driving by. And yet, here was silly me, walking, hopping, sweating, and tripping over my one skate trying to catch up. But they were too many blocks ahead of me.

"J.D.! Slow down J.D.!" (J.D. was my brother's nickname; sorry, I don't think I've mentioned that yet). Anyways, I kept calling his name, but he wouldn't turn around to look at me. Finally, Willis heard me and looked back. "Looky here Jonathan! Your little baby brother wants you to slow down and hold his little baby hand! Wah, wah!" At first, I was angry at being called a baby. But then, I could feel my heart breaking when I realized that my brother was not sticking up for me. At that moment, I felt rejected and abandoned. I gave up trying to follow them, and I somehow got back home. I walked the whole way. "I never want to see anymore stupid skates!" I angrily yelled into my pillow. That day, I learned that I needed to be tough and fend for myself so I wouldn't be embarrassed again. This new attitude followed me to the fourth grade. They didn't know it, but a young monster was about to walk through their doors!

Next Time…

After stealing from people, seeing another deadly accident, and being rejected by my brother, I toughened up on the inside. You seem like you may have been through something similar. If so, I hope that you find someone that you can open up to about what you are feeling. That's the best way to avoid becoming violent and rowdy like I did. When I meet you again, I'll give you some highlights from that time of my life. And remember, we all have our own stories. Don't be afraid to share yours!

Questions to Discuss

1. Is it nice to laugh when bad things happen to other people?

2. In addition to stealing, what other bad thing did Jonathan do? (think about Miss Heraldine)

3. Why didn't Miss Virginia want to fight with David's mom?

4. Should you do dangerous things just to be cool?

5. How did David feel when his brother got new friends?

A Young Boy Named David
Book 7
Young and Tough

Written By
David M. Smith

A Young Boy Named David Book 7: Young and Tough

Written By: David M. Smith

Characters

- David – me
- Leon – bully
- Mr. Butler
- Rhonda
- James Johnson
- James Wilkinson
- Mr. B, Mrs. B, and Baby B – family of rulers (you'll see)

Chapter 1: Where My Fighting Started

My fighting history in school dates all the way back to pre-K. The portable building where my mom dropped me off and left me in that strange place. I was so very afraid, the first time around any kids and this weird feeling started creeping up in me.

"Please mom! Don't leave me here!" I begged her. But she did. I looked around at all the faces of these kids that I didn't know, and I just felt so angry about the whole thing. There was a big chubby kid that sat in front of me, and he was the class bully. Because he was bigger than everyone else, he would take our toys and push us around. I couldn't wait to get back home and away from this scary kid.

I was being bullied before I even knew what that meant. Then one day, Leon (the bully) walked up and took away my favorite box of crayons. "These are mine now!" he growled. To my surprise, and to everyone else's, I got so mad at this that I pulled back and whopped Leon so hard that he fell over and hit his face on a desk! We couldn't believe it! Little David had taken down the big bad bully! The amount of respect and fear I got from the other kids in the class became something I was determined to have all throughout my school days.

Fast forward to the fourth grade, and I had become a young and tough boy ready to act up and show out! Not having any guidance in my life was causing my behavior to go down the drain. That's what happens when there's no adult taking an interest in raising you to be a good person. Have you gone through this? I hope not. But if so, I pray that one of your teachers steps up to fill this role for you. This happened to me with Mr. Butler. I'll tell you more about him later. For now, I have some more stories to tell about the beginning of my school fighting career!

In Mr. Butler's class, there were 14 students. All were boys, except for Rhonda, the only girl in the group. "You boys don't scare me at all! Don't try to mess with me, or I'll pop you in the head!" she declared to all of us one day. I stood up and said, "we aren't afraid of no girl! Bring it on, Rho-" POP!!! You guessed it...I got popped in the head by Rhonda! As tough as my life at home was making me, I knew to leave Rhonda alone! In fact, we actually became close friends after this. Really, Rhonda was cool with all the guys in the class. Even though she still sucked her thumb, she had proven her toughness, and we never teased her about it.

Now to tell you about Mr. Butler. I can still remember the first day in his class. "Alright kids.

Listen up," he said to all of us in his big booming voice. I tried to listen, but I was distracted by his size and full beard and mustache. He continued, "this is my class, and I'm the one in charge. Don't you forget it. Let me introduce you to my family." He then went up to the board and grabbed three rulers.

"Say hello to Mr. B, Mrs. B, and Baby B." All three rulers were different sizes, and he said that he would only have to use them if we acted up or got out of hand. Let's just say that I became very familiar with Mr. Butler's "family"!

Mr. Butler had an interesting way of dealing with us. It turns out that all the rough and troubled kids got sent to his class. And we all had built up anger and stress from our lives at home, which meant we were always getting into fights. Here's what's crazy…*Mr. Butler would let us fight!* This created a system among us. The kids who were good fighters and won a lot were the ones who were seen as the top class, the kids you didn't mess with.

Right away, they could tell that I would fight. "You know why they call me Monster Mash?" I said, trying to brag to my classmates. "Why?" a kid named James said. "Because a monster mashed you in the head and made you stupid?" This got a huge laugh out of everyone. But all it did was make me very angry. "No, James, it's because if you mash the wrong button, I'll go monster all over your dumb self!"

Well, James had officially challenged me in front of everyone. I could tell that he wanted to take the spot as the number one tough guy. Little did I know that this would lead to an intense battle between him and me to find out who was really the toughest in Mr. Butler's class!

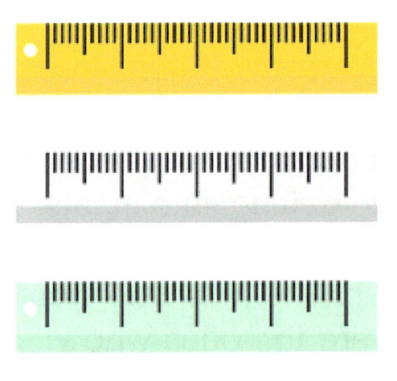

Chapter 2: A Boy Named James

I don't know what James was going through in his life, but I do know that this was a very dark time in my life. I was so full of anger at home because of my mom's problems getting worse, my brother ditching me for his new friends, and seeing so many terrible accidents with my own two eyes. So when I got to school, I was already in a mean, fighting mood, and anything could set me over the edge. I had developed a temper. I would go off fast on someone. Usually, it was James Johnson who I fought the most. Which was surprising when you realize that James was a really big guy! In fact, we called him the Incredible Hulk because when he got angry his face would get dark and he would sometimes break things.

But that didn't scare me. I was just mad that he tried to be a bully and take over the classroom. Back in those days, I was ready to fight just about anyone!

"Come on guys, who do you think would win in a fight...a Monster or a Hulk?" James asked the class one day. I remember us all standing by the door, probably because class was almost over. Something came over me, and I just snapped. "Why don't you stop asking and come fight me to find out?" I yelled. That started my first real fight in school! James came rushing at me full force. My eyes got big. I didn't expect him to come at me so hard! "David, look out!" Rhonda cried out, but it was too late. James, as tall as he was, got to me in just two steps, lifted me up, and was trying to squeeze the life out of me, like I was a lemon!

"Let me go!" I struggled to say. Then I raised my hand back and knocked James right in the face. BAM! BAM! I hit him twice, and he fell back and let me go. I hit him hard enough to make him run to the back of the classroom and stop trying to out-tough me. Mr. Butler, who had been watching the whole fight go down, stood up and said, "well, now that you guys got that out of your system, maybe we can start acting a bit more civilized." Wow! There's no way a teacher would have that reaction nowadays. I actually don't like the idea of kids fighting in school. In the end, you don't prove anything, and you just end up getting hurt.

I don't want you guys to fight like I did. If you have problems at home or have issues with someone in your class, go to one of your counselors for help. That way, you might avoid going through what happened in my next fight. Interestingly enough, it was with another kid named James!

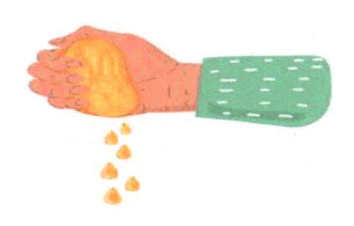

Chapter 3: The Other James

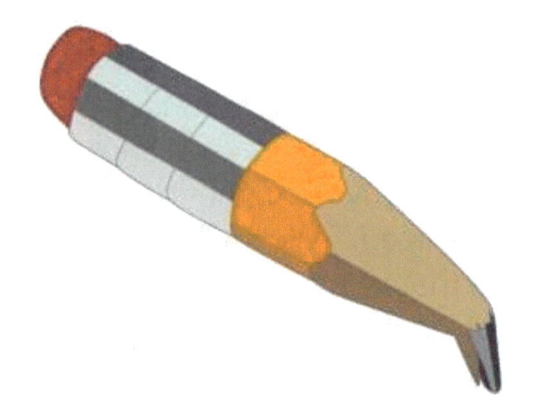

My fights continued, and it seemed like everyone named James had it out for me! I was definitely angrier at this other James, because that day in class, James Wilkinson brought up my brother's death. "Hey David? Whatever happened to your little brother, huh? Where are you guys hiding him?" he said one day. I couldn't believe what I heard him say. "James. Be very careful about what you say next," I said in a low, angry voice. "Awww, the little baby Monster Mash is gonna cry! Hahaha!"

At this, some of the other kids began laughing with James, and I could no longer hold back my feelings. I loved my brother Larry so much, and when we lost him to a disease, it made me go into a very dark place. Now, it was being brought up as a rude joke, and people were laughing at him. What was I supposed to do?

I'll tell you what…I should have gone to a teacher. When you're upset like that, you need an adult to help you make a good decision. That will prevent you from doing something violent or mean, which will only make the situation worse anyways.

Also, from the viewpoint of James, please know that it's never good to make fun of someone's family, especially someone they have lost. The pain of that loss can activate emotions in that person that are hard for them to control. And boy, is that what happened to me!

"James, I'm going to tell you one more time. Stop. Talking. About. My. Brother!!" I was standing up this time, staring him down with the meanest glare I could come up with. It didn't work. "Why doesn't your brother come over here and stop me? Oh, right! He can't, because he's-"

I didn't dare let him finish that sentence. I had been drawing at my desk, so my pencil was nearby. I grabbed it and ran up to James. He was still laughing at his dumb "joke", so he didn't see me coming.

I raised my hand back, put all my force into it, and slammed it down into his shoulder! You have never heard a little boy scream and yell so loud! Of all the fights we had in Mr. Butler's class, this one made him leap out of his seat and get involved. I guess he drew the line at breaking off a pencil in a kid's shoulder! "David Smith! What in the world did you do??" he shouted at me. Forget Mr. B, Mrs. B, or Baby B…he looked mad enough to come at me all by himself!

James ended up in the nurse's office, and I was sent home and not allowed to come back to school for the rest of the week. I don't want you to react to situations the way I did. But I can tell you that no one ever made fun of Little Larry again!

Next Time…

Like I've said already, fighting is never the answer. But at that time in my life, it's all I knew how to do. My anger was growing and growing, and the only people I felt like I could take it out on were my classmates. Because I was so tough, I won many of my fights. But I quickly learned that you can't win them all! Come back next time to hear about some of the battles that didn't turn out the way I had hoped! And remember, we all have our own stories. Don't be afraid to tell yours!

Questions to Discuss

1. How did you feel when your parents left you at school for the first time?

2. Do you think it was right for Mr. Butler to let his students fight each other?

3. Have you ever been bullied like David was? How did it make you feel?

4. Is it right to make fun of someone's dead family member?

5. Was it right for David to fight back when he was upset?

A Young Boy Named David
Book 8
You Can't Win Them All!

Written By
David M. Smith

A Young Boy Named David Book 8: You Can't Win Them All!

Written By: David M. Smith

Characters

- David – me
- Mr. Butler
- Ellis
- James Johnson
- Rimando
- Nurse Mack

Chapter 1: A Tie in the Bathroom

There was a change coming to Mr. Butler's class. The fights were getting out of hand in the classroom, so he gave us all a new location to battle it out. He said to us one day, "from now on, I don't want any more fights in this class. If you have to beat each other up, go do it in the bathroom. You can come back once you've finished." This surprised us. He was basically encouraging us to fight! Thankfully, teachers nowadays would never suggest something like this. But hey, it was a different time back then! The teacher could whip you and not get into trouble.

This new change didn't stop the fights at all. They just kept happening, day after day. I still remember my first bathroom battle with a kid named Ellis, whose nickname was Frog. This was because he liked to jump on people and hit them and he had a funny shaped forehead. The thing was, he only jumped on people that he thought couldn't beat him up. Then one day, he decided to get froggy with me. He made the big mistake of jumping on me!

"Get up David! You just got jumped by the Frog!" Somehow, nicknames are less cool when you use them on yourself. Anyways, this sudden attack had me pretty upset. "Don't you know that monsters eat frogs?!" I said, trying to make up a corny joke of my own. Then I shoved him off of me and was about to start hitting him back (don't try this at home) when Mr. Butler grabbed us by the arms and led us to the bathroom.

"You guys got something to prove? Then go ahead! You're in the right place now. Go on!" Wow! He was giving us permission to go crazy on each other! We both were so upset at that point that he didn't need to tell us twice. He just stood by and watched us go at it.

Oh, and I forgot to mention Mr. Butler's one rule for these bathroom fights. We could only leave when one or both of us agreed to stop fighting. Of course, no kid wanted the shame of going back to the classroom as a loser, so we would fight like Pit Bulls to come out on top!

The battle was now on! Ellis would throw a punch, then I would throw a punch. I would grab Ellis, then he would grab me. This went on for a few minutes. "Come on David," Ellis huffed. I could tell he was getting tired. "Give up already!" "And lose to a kid who calls himself Frog? No way, buddy!" Finally, we both ran out of steam. We were breathing heavily like we had just run five miles. At this point, we had to hold each other up just to stand.

Mr. Butler walked up to us and asked, "Are we done here?" Ellis and I looked at one another, and we honestly could not pick a clear winner. Both of us had hit the other person several times, both of our clothes were ripped, and we were both exhausted. I had a swollen lip and Ellis has a swollen eye. I spoke up for us and answered Mr. Butler. "We're going to agree that it was a tie." "Looks that way to me as well," our teacher replied. "Now let's get back to class."

You know what's funny? Even after our battle, me and Ellis actually became friends that day! That's more than what I can say about these next two fights.

Chapter 2: Almost Thrown Out of the Third Floor Window!

Every kid looked forward to the talent show. It was the one time when we got to talk about something good in our lives. I had a couple toys that I was proud to show off. One of them was my football. It was basically the only thing I had from my dad. Even though I didn't see him regularly, the football was awesome!

"This is what the professionals use in the NFL," I bragged to the class. "I've been practicing my throwing, and I can toss my football further than any kid at my house!" (I didn't think I needed to mention that, aside from my brother, I was the only kid at the house!) I happened to notice that while I said this, my rival James Johnson looked at me and rolled his eyes. I guess he didn't believe me. No problem...I had something in store for him when it was *his* turn to share!

A few turns later, James was up in front of the class showing off some of his army man figures. Now was my chance to get on his nerves. "So basically," I said out loud, "you play with army dolls?" Boy, this got some giggles out of everyone! James was the only one not laughing, though. This time, there was no bathroom fight. He dropped his toys and came at me right then and there! "My brother is in the army! Don't you dare make fun of my army toys!"

I had made the mistake of teasing James about something that was really important to him, like how someone had been making fun of my lost little brother. And as hard as I had fought that day, James was about to fight me just as hard!

Mr. Butler's class was on the third floor, and we happened to fight our way over by the window. So imagine my surprise when that crazy boy James picked me up and *actually tried to throw me out of it!* At this point, I was kicking and hitting him like a madman. What would you do if you were about to be thrown down from 30 feet or more up in the air?

"Are you crazy?? Let me go!" I could barely even shout because he was holding me so tight that I couldn't catch a breath. His face was turning colors like the Incredible Hulk, huffing and puffing spit. Mr. Butler and the rest of the class were caught off guard by how quick James had charged me. In our struggle, we had knocked over desks and chairs, making it hard for anyone to get to us and break us up.

Eventually, the pounding I was giving to his face caused him to loosen his grip on me, just enough for me to break free and get away from him! By now, Mr. Butler had made his way to us, and he dragged both of us to the principal's office. Once again, I got suspended. I guess I started the whole thing by making fun of his army toy.

    I learned that people can be very attached to family members and memories in their lives. So you really need to be careful about making fun of something. You never know the emotional meaning it may have, or the violent reaction you may trigger by calling it out.

Chapter 3: My One Lost Fight

The memory of the fight I lost in Mr. Butler's class is still fresh in my mind. It was to Rimando, one of the grossest kids among all of us! First, he sucked his thumb all day long, which made it look white and sore, let alone the nasty smell! And to make matters worse, he had a stuttering problem, which would cause him to sometimes spit on you as he tried to get his words out. This really got on my nerves, especially since he sat right next to me!

One day, I couldn't take it anymore! "Rimando, if you don't get your stanky breath out of my face, I'm gonna knock that thumb right out of your mouth!" I yelled. The whole class looked at us, wanting to see what Rimando would do. He was normally a smart talker, always trying to prove himself right and talk down to the other students. But this time, he was calm. All he said was, "Ok, David. I'll back away from you. I'm sorry to have bothered you." We all were shocked by this response!

It actually made me feel like my title of the best fighter at school had caused him to back down. I felt really proud at that moment. But little did I know that Rimando wasn't going to drop the issue that easily! He had actually been very embarrassed about what I said about him, and his way of getting back at me was hidden from sight under his desk.

I was also caught off guard because his sneak attack was going to take place in the classroom, and not in the bathroom where our fights were supposed to take place. I could tell that he was playing with something in his hands, but I didn't give it a second thought. My friend Ellis, however, saw that something was up, and at least he tried to warn me.

"Hey David," he whispered. "I think Rimando is planning something. Stay ready." However, I ignored him. After all, what could he do from his desk? Well, I was about to find out! "Hey David! How does my breath smell now?" Rimando said to me. Confused by the question, I turned around, then...

BOOM!! Rimando had hit me across the face with a quarter in his hand! I had never felt pain like that before, and no one in my class had seen it either. Their mouths were hanging open, and they kept saying, "your nose! Wow, look at your nose!"

When Mr. Butler rushed me to the nurse's office, I finally did get to look at my nose. I almost passed out from the sight of it, and I had to let out a scared scream! "Oh, my goodness! Is my nose broken? Will I ever be able to smell again?" I asked Nurse Mack. Usually, I sent kids to her office; I wasn't used to being in there myself! "You'll be fine after it sets, David. Keep this ice on it for now."

After losing a fight like this, the game was changed. I thought long and hard about whether or not I should give up my fighting days. I didn't know if my body could take any more of this! I do appreciate the friends I gained in the fourth grade. Many of them were kids I had fought with, and we ended up having a close bond. Some of them even offered to fight Rimando back for me. But I was slowly coming to see that revenge and violence wasn't addressing my true issues.

I started to remember what Miss Virginia had said about my mom. Maybe it was time to stop fighting others and start trying to get better. I know what I needed…a real family to give me guidance and help. So that's what I started looking for.

Next Time...

Enough about my school days! Next time we meet, I want to tell you about some more things that happened to me at home and some of the people that entered my life. I was hoping to find some father figure, brother, grandma, uncle, somebody to help me grow and teach me how to be a good person. Many of you may be looking for the same thing. If so, never stop looking for it! It's there for all of us. And it might be someone you would least expect! Also, remember that all of us have a story. Don't be afraid to tell yours!

Questions to Discuss

1. How did David and Ellis become friends?

2. Should David have made fun of James Johnson's army toys?

3. How did that make James J. feel?

4. Was it right for James J. to attack David?

5. Do you think it was a good thing that David didn't want his friends to get back at Rimando?

A Young Boy Named David
Book 9
Looking For Family

Written By
David M. Smith

A Young Boy Named David Book 9: Looking For Family

Written By: David M. Smith

Characters

- David – me
- Mary Matthews - grammy
- Sylvia – mom
- The nuns
- My F.A.T.H.E.R.

Chapter 1: Brief Memory of My Grandmother

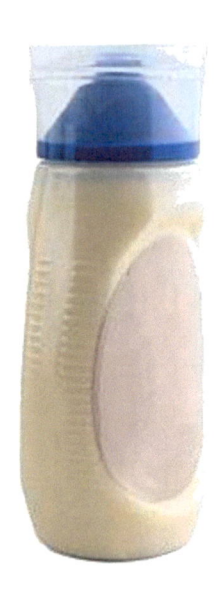

My grandmother, Mary Matthews, was in my life for a few years, but I don't have many memories of her. I wish I had more. I can remember one time when I was over at her house, and I was really hungry. "Grammy," I called her. "There's nothing to eat, and I'm starving!" "Baby," she said to me. "If you use your imagination, you'll always find something to make. Here, let me show you." So I followed her to the kitchen and watched her make me a mayonnaise sandwich! I never would have thought to make that. She taught me that day to always make the most of any situation. And that mayonnaise sandwich was absolutely delicious!

Another memory I had of her was when I would go over to her house in the middle of the winter. In Baltimore, this time of year was extremely cold! To make it even worse, she didn't have an extra bed, so when my brother and I would go to visit, we had to sleep on the floor. And that floor was hard and cold! "Jonathan, I'm going to freeze solid! How many coats do you have over you?" "I don't know, maybe like ten?" he answered. "But stop talking to me. You're wasting heat! I'm freezing!" I didn't think that was true, but I left him alone. I wondered how my grandmother could survive living in a house that cold! She was definitely a tough lady.

Later, I asked my mom for more details about my grandma since I didn't really know a lot about her. "Hey mom? I want to know more about grandma Mary. Can you tell me about her?" "Of course, David. Your grandmother Mary was a sweetheart. She was the spiritual leader of the family. She loved God and taught us how to pray." "How many of you guys are there?" I wondered. "She had seven children. I'm the oldest girl," my mom answered. "And you want to know something, David? When you were really little, she would pray for you every day, asking you to grow up to be big and strong."

Hearing that warmed my heart! Grandma Mary, thank you for the prayers. I believe that because of your care and interest, there was always a spark of good in me, just waiting to come out.

At this point in my life, looking back, I can say that it finally is shining the way you always knew it could. And reader, there's a light in you, too! All you need is a few good people in your life to bring it out. Don't stop looking until you find them!

Chapter 2: The Nuns Across the Street

Another good influence I had around me to fight off the darkness were the friendly nuns across the street. Although I was still young, I felt like things I saw in my life were straight from a PG-13 movie! But whenever I was at the church, I felt closer to a higher power that was pulling me into a life full of faith and goodness.

At the house, no one hardly ever talked about God, so I didn't really know much about God or religion. I often thought that He wasn't there. If that were true, why was my life so rotten and bad? I've come to learn that the only person to blame for bad things that happen are the bad people that did them. Living your life blaming God or yourself for these things will only hold you back. In addition to spiritual lessons, I also had fun hanging out at the church when the nuns would let me come over. I would go into the sanctuary and kneel down, get holy water, and pray. I would get to work there on Saturdays when they had bingo night, and the old ladies who would come to play would tip me money!

These people were happy, faithful, and nice to me. They treated each other with respect, they didn't use bad language, and they lived by the Bible. I imagined that my grandmother would have gotten along well with them. That's when it all hit me; this was the family I was looking for! They accepted me and made me feel welcome, and the lessons they taught me helped me to make sense of the world around me.

The nuns at the church taught me how to pray and, more important, how to live. I got to feel like a normal kid when I was around them. They fed me normal food, and they even had some nice clothes to give me every now and then. This was like my home away from home, and I'm so grateful that it was there at the time when I needed direction and guidance. I hope that if you have a troubled background, you come to find your home away from home too!

Chapter 3: Where is My Father?

f.a.t.h.e.r.

You know what's funny? Not laugh out loud funny, but funny as in "wow, are you serious?" What's funny is that I spent all this time looking for family, and the whole time my real dad only lived ten miles away! I tried to find a father in Mr. Blato (the house owner), my mom's brothers, and my brother. But none of them ever really filled that role the way I needed them to.

I have to be honest with you...I grew up in a time and place where most black fathers did not stay with their families. The men would run around town getting in trouble with all the girls, but as soon as they got pregnant, the men would leave. Not only did that happen to me and my brother, but all the kids in Mr. Butler's class went through the same thing. This was really the source of our behavior problems. We were walking around blaming ourselves for our families being broken, which caused us to be attacked by thoughts of confusion and anger. These emotional attacks on the inside would make us physically attack people on the outside. How else could you explain eight-year-old kids fighting each other on a daily basis?

I'd love to say that this was only a problem with my generation, but I look around and see a lot of kids today going through the same thing I did. And I know the question you're always asking yourself: "Where is my father?" Well, here's the answer.

Your F.A.T.H.E.R. is anyone who: is Friendly to you, has Authority, Teaches you, Helps you, makes an Effort to get your trust, and Respects you. In this way, anyone can be a father. For me, Ms. Drake, Ms. Turner, and Mrs. Salem were fathers. Mr. Owens and Mr. Butler were fathers. For a short time, Mr. Blato was a father. So you see, it's not about who you're related to. It's about who puts in the work to show you that fatherly love.

Like my grandmother and the nuns taught me to do, I will continue to pray for you to find the father you have been searching for, no matter who or where he or she may be!

Hopefully, they are closer than you think. Oh, and when you do find them...don't be too afraid to let them in! That's the only way they'll be able to help.

Next Time...

Isn't it true that our lives are filled with good times, bad times, and funny times? Well, I've got plenty of those stories to tell the next time I see you! I look forward to meeting up with you again. In the meantime, remember that all of us have our own stories. Don't be afraid to share yours!

Questions to Discuss

1. What did Grandma Mary do that had a positive effect on David?

2. How did the nuns treat David?

3. What kind of activities did he help out with at the church?

4. How far away did David's father live?

5. Who can be your father?

A Young Boy Named David
Book 10
The Good, the Bad, and the Karate

Written By

David M. Smith

A Young Boy Named David Book 10: The Good, the Bad, and the Karate

Written By: David M. Smith

Characters

- David – me
- Mr. Teddy
- Mr. Teddy's kids and mother
- Jonathan – older brother
- Willis Humphrey
- Mr. German Shepherd
- Mr. Conway/Karate Kid
- Tweety Bird

Chapter 1: Mr. Teddy

Mr. Teddy didn't live at the house, but he was over so much that it felt that way. He had two kids, but he would leave them behind with his mother and come to our part of town to spend his money. He seemed to really have a crush on Miss Precious. I didn't agree with him leaving his children so often, but I have to say that he did show me kindness when he would visit, and that was a good feeling. One time, he offered me to go with him back to his house so I could hang out with his family. This was a good feeling because I never traveled out of the city.

It turns out that they were some of the nicest people I ever met! His two kids were actually way older than I thought. I think they were in their twenties or thirties. They both had disabilities, which in their case meant that they talked just a little bit differently and thought just a little bit slower than other people. Mr. Teddy explained this to me on the drive up there.

"Do me a favor, Monster Mash. Don't feel like you have to talk to my kids any differently than anyone else. They can hear and speak fine; it just might take them slightly longer to process everything." "You got it Mr. Teddy," I replied. This is a very good lesson that he was teaching me. I learned that you should treat everyone the same without being rude or mean to them for no reason, especially if they have a disability.

I actually really liked his children! I don't remember their names, but I remember them being the funniest adult man and woman I had ever been around! Mr. Teddy's mom was a sweetheart too. She cleaned up after my dirty dishes and clothes without complaining. I think she was excited to have a young kid nearby to baby around, and I didn't mind. It was like having my grandma back!

One more memory I have from Mr. Teddy is how he taught me to cook eggs. Doing it his way involved flipping it a certain way several times and watching the heat real closely. To this day, that lesson is still coming in handy when it comes time for breakfast!

I am so glad that Mr. Teddy helped me to have these good times and happy memories. It was a welcome change from all the bad things and people at Mosher Street…like Mr. German Shepherd. When it was time to leave, I didn't want to go.

Chapter 2: Mr. German Shepherd

There weren't that many places that I would hang out at outside of the house. It would either be at the church, Willis Humphrey's house (they had moved up the street), or around the corner on Druid Hills Avenue with a kid named Snooda, Willis' nephew's house. That was where me and my brother came to meet a mean man who called himself Mr. German Shepherd.

I know what you might be thinking…where were all these grown men getting these ridiculous nicknames?? I don't know, but it wasn't just his name that stood out. It was also the kind of games he taught us and the way he treated us that I really remember.

"Alright kiddos, let me teach you all how to play cards and shoot dice," he said to us. "Umm, I thought those were grown up games," I said. He gave me a look that said he wanted me to shut up and let him do his thing. I later found out why. He wanted to teach us how to play so he could make us think we were really good and cheat us out of our money!

He would even yell and threaten us in order to scare us, or should I say, *try* to scare us. We never saw him as a threat, but this still was not a good environment for us to be around.

Mr. German Shepherd who lived on Druid Hills Avenue was related to Humphrey, who he met Lilda who had three children of her own. She was Willis' older sister. Lilda would play games with us too. The games would usually start early in the morning, and he would come downstairs wearing his hat to the side, dress socks up to his knees, and slippers on his feet, as he bopped across the floor.

Mr. German Shepherd was the kind of person who would try to trick people out of their money. This caused him to get on a lot of people's nerves. "Willis, what happened to you?" Jonathan said one day. We could tell that Willis had been fighting with someone. "I was playing dice with Mr. G.S. and he tried to cheat me out of my cash. I called him out on it and shoved him. He didn't like that too much, and we battled for a little bit." "I can't believe he would fight a kid!" I said. But really, he fought lots of people. There were a lot of other people at the house on Druid Hills, including a man named John.

John had a disease that would cause his body to lock up and stop moving without any control. I'm not proud of this now, but we used to laugh and tease him when this happened. Not only was it disrespectful to him as an adult, but it was really mean to treat him like that when he couldn't do anything about his problem. If you know someone that has a condition that they can't control, please don't make fun of them.

And definitely don't do what Mr. German Shepherd did. One day, we were hanging out with Willis, and John happened to be there eating a bowl of cereal. All of a sudden, his body locked up, and the bowl, as well as John, fell to the floor. His eyes were wide open and his tongue was sticking out, and we just busted out laughing at this.

"What's going on down there?!" Mr. German Shepherd screamed as he came down. Then he saw John on the floor, and instead of trying to help him, he grabbed him and started hitting him and shouting at him! "Get up and stop pretending! I told you not to do this anymore! Get off of that floor!" This made us stop laughing and feel bad for John. "What kind of mean person would treat someone on the ground like that?" I said.

Let's see: probably someone who taught adult games to kids, tried to cheat them out of their money, and fought with everyone he met. There were a lot of bad things I saw Mr. German Shepherd say and do, and I actually tried my best to make sure that I didn't grow up to be a mean old man like him! Did I mention, he also was a loan shark.

Chapter 3: Mr. Conway, the "Karate Kid"

I also have to mention that there was another man in my life at that time who was a good influence like Mr. Teddy was. That was Mr. Conway, or as we called him, the Karate Kid. He was a big, heavy man who loved karate and was also in a band with Mr. Blato and some other of his friends. They would sometimes have concerts in the backyard at 507 Mosher Street. Sometimes all through the night.

We called him Karate Kid because he would always do chops and kicks around us to make us laugh, and he would also scream as if he was fighting in a martial arts match. Bruce Lee! "HIIIIYYYAAAAA!! WAAAAH HAAAHH!!" This had me laughing so hard! Seeing a big man do those moves and make those sounds was the funniest thing I had ever seen.

He was dating Tweety Bird at the time, and I can remember her running around with him chasing after her. I couldn't tell if they were playing or fighting, but it was still pretty hilarious to look at. "Get back here before I chop kick you, woman!" he would say. "You have to catch me first, Karate Boy," she said back to him. "Hey, he's not a Karate Boy, he's the Karate Kid!" I shouted without thinking. Oops! Now they know that I was watching them! But it was ok. Mr. Conway just turned to look at me, and he winked, letting me know that he was happy I liked to use his nickname.

I say that Karate Kid was a good influence on me, but really, I just remember him making me laugh and smile. Really, that was important for me. At that time, we were poor, my brother was making new friends, and I was getting into fights at school. I believe that being able to come home and know that good laughs were waiting for me kept the darkness inside me from coming all the way out. Like they say, laughter really is the best medicine! If you're going through a rough patch in your life, try to find someone or something funny to make you feel better!

Next Time…

It wasn't just adults that I was around all the time. There were also some new kids that I became friends with. We had plenty of adventures that ended up teaching me important lessons, and I can't wait to tell you about them when I see you all again! I'm looking forward to our next story time, buddies. And don't forget that we all have our own special stories. Remember to share yours!

Questions to Discuss

1. Did David talk to Mr. Teddy's kids differently due to their disabilities?

2. Was it right for Mr. Teddy to leave behind his children so often?

3. What should you do if an adult tries to teach you something wrong?

4. Is it right to laugh and make fun of someone's medical problem?

5. How can laughter help you to get through rough times?

A Young Boy Named David
Book II
Making New Friends

Written By
David M. Smith

A Young Boy Named David Book 11: Making New Friends

Written By: David M. Smith

Characters

- David – me
- Jonathan – older brother
- Willis Humphrey
- Stella Humphrey
- "Snooda" Humphrey

Chapter 1: Jonathan, Come Back!

As time went on, I could tell that my brother was slowly drifting away from me. We shared a room, but he spent so much time hanging out with his friends in the streets that I barely ever saw him. "Hey Jonathan! Where ya been?" I asked when he got back really late. Without even looking me in the eyes, he just said, "whatever, I'm tired. We'll talk in the morning." Well, morning came, but when I looked over, he was nowhere to be seen. Times like this made me feel like I didn't even have a brother at all.

Sometimes, Jonathan's friends would come to the house to get him. His main friend was Willis Humphrey. Let me tell you a little bit about this kid. For starters, he still sucked his thumb! He was a teenager, and his parents basically let him do whatever he wanted. I don't know what Jonathan saw in him, but all I noticed when he came over was his beautiful sister, Stella!

One day, Willis came over and whistled from the bottom of our window to get Jonathan's attention. When I looked out to see who it was...there was Stella, standing right next to her brother and looking up at me with those big brown eyes! "Hey David!" she smiled and waved at me, and I thought I was going to faint and fall right out of that window! "Where's your brother?" Willis yelled up at me. "I, um, he's about to..." I could barely talk straight with Stella there. Finally, Jonathan spoke up. "Ignore my weird brother. I'll be right out," he replied.

As the three of them left to do who knows what, I had one question that I couldn't get out of my mind...am I in love with Stella?!

Chapter 2: The Humphreys

What does an eight-year-old know about love? All I knew was that I wanted to get closer to Stella, I would need to get closer to the Humphrey family. Which meant that I needed to convince my brother to let me come with him to their house.

"Jonathan?" I asked my older brother. "What do you want?" he replied. "What kind of things do you do when you hang out with Willis?" "We do big boy stuff." What did that mean? I couldn't be ok with such a short answer. But I realized that if I kept asking about it, I would just get on his nerves. So I decided to try something.

"Hmm. Sounds cool." That's it. I tried to act like I didn't care about it anymore, which took everything I had! A few minutes went by. We were just sitting there, not saying anything. I didn't ask him another question. Just when I was about to give up on my plan, he broke the silence. "Alright, I'll tell you what we do. But you have to promise me that you won't tell momma." "Promise!" I said, probably a bit too excitedly.

Jonathan continued, "one thing we do is steal candy bars from the corner store. Stella will go in as a distraction, keeping the clerk busy. Then me and Willis will go in at separate times and put a couple candy bars in our pockets." "Whoa. Don't you guys ever feel guilty doing that?" I was surprised to hear that even Stella helped them to rob these stores. Would I also have to start stealing to have any chance of her liking me? And would it be even worth it?

"Don't be a baby, David! You're starting to sound like Snooda," my brother said. "Uh, what is a Snooda?" I was so confused! "Not what, who. That's what we call Frederick, Willis and Stella's younger nephew. He's about your age, and he's always trying to talk us out of stealing."

This could be my chance! An idea was forming in my head. "Hey! Why don't you let me come over to hang out with Snooda? That way I can keep him busy so he won't bother you guys when you go out!" "You know what? That's a good idea, Monster Mash! I'm gonna bring you with me the next time I go over there."

Yes! My plan worked! I was on my way to getting closer to my crush, Stella. I just hoped that this Snooda kid wasn't too weird!

Chapter 3: Little Frederick

It turns out that Snooda was quite an interesting person! "Hey! Why do they call you Snooda anyways?" I asked him. "That's easy. It's because I'm a sneaky dude-a!" I laughed at this. Not only was Snooda a jokester, but he was good with money. In fact, I never knew him to have less than five bucks in his pocket at any time! What made him different from his brother and sister was that he didn't steal. He earned his money through working jobs in the neighborhood and winning games.

Thankfully, his hard-working attitude rubbed off on me, and I began to work hard and make my own money, too. We also spent time together working at the church. We had a healthy competition about who could earn the most money. "How much you got, Monster Mash?" he wondered. "Let's see," I said. "This week I made $25 dollars. What about you?" He just looked at me and grinned. "Oh, not much. Just $50!"

It felt like he was bragging, so we started pretending to fight. After all, you can't go all out in a church! I ended up forgetting about my crush on Stella because I was so focused on having a best friend of my own in Snooda! He was such a bright spot in my life back then, which made what happened to him extremely sad.

The entire Humphrey family would be lost to a house fire in the near future. Me and Jonathan would be heartbroken over this. We had found friends that were helping us to escape the darkness, but then just like that they were gone. There was no one to blame. There was no explanation. They were just...gone.

Maybe this has happened to you. Maybe one day you heard about an accident that suddenly changed your world forever. If that's the case, you need to talk to someone about how you feel. And I mean how you *really* feel. So many kids have bottled up their emotions when bad things happen, and it leads to them being swallowed up by anger. I lived through this, and trust me, it isn't fun.

You won't always be prepared for pain. But if you make yourself aware of your pain, and you share your pain, that is the best way to truly care for your pain.

Next Time...

Losing Snooda would be tough for me. I wish I would have known you back then! You're a great listener, and that would have helped me to deal with what I was feeling on the inside. Instead, I chose another path to try to make things better, a path that other kids at school and in the neighborhood were going to: anger. It didn't work for us, though. That's why I want to talk to you about this next time; so you know what not to do to handle tough times. Also, remember that we all have a story to share. Don't be afraid to tell yours!

Questions to Discuss

1. Have you ever felt like you were in love before?

2. Should you do bad things just for someone to like you?

3. Would you rather steal money or earn money?

4. Has anyone you know ever been in a bad accident?

5. If you knew David back then, what could you say to comfort him?

A Young Boy Named David
Book 12
Angry Kids!

Written By
David M. Smith

A Young Boy Named David Book 12: Angry Kids!

Written By: David M. Smith

Characters

- David – me
- Mr. Butler
- James Wilkinson
- Anthony
- Angry gang of kids

Chapter 1: Trying to Fight the Teacher!

Have you ever felt like life was moving too fast? Like you didn't have enough time to figure just what was going on? I can understand, because that's how I felt! I was losing people I cared about, and it was changing my mood into being angry all the time. This followed me to school and affected my behavior. What I didn't realize was that these things were happening to other kids as well. And it was making them feel the same way as me. This meant that there were a lot of angry kids walking around, and what do you think would happen when they got together? Fights!

Eventually, I had fought almost all the kids in my class, and I wanted a new challenge. That's when I got the dumb idea of trying to take on Mr. Butler! Let me tell you how that went.

"Ok class, settle down. It's time to begin today's lesson," Mr. Butler said to the class. For some reason, that morning I didn't want to be told what to do. "You know what?" I said, interrupting him. "Why don't I teach today? Our first lesson will be how to survive without adults!" Oh, did this make Mr. Butler angry! "David Smith, have you lost your mind? You sit down this instant!" As he said this, he walked over to my desk to stand over me until I listened to him. I didn't like that too much, and a crazy thought came to my mind.

Once he got close enough, I jumped out of my seat really quick and shoved Mr. Butler with all of my might! This was the new challenge I was looking for: trying to fight my teacher! But I had no idea how strong this man was. First of all, my attempt to knock him down was an epic fail. Next, he grabbed me by the collar and lifted me straight up into the air!

I kicked out with my feet and fell to the floor, and that's when Mr. Butler pinned me to the ground. I tried to move and get free, but he was holding onto me tight with his big strong hands. I could still breathe, but it was getting harder and harder for me to break out from under him.

The kids in the class were all shocked to see what was happening! If kids were fighting, you would go and tell the teacher. But what are you supposed to do when the teacher is *in* the fight? I realized that I had bitten off way more than I could chew! Once he knew that I had learned my lesson, he got off of me and let me up. I got back in my seat and didn't look at anyone the rest of the day.

What happened that day didn't stop us from fighting each other, but no one ever challenged Mr. Butler again!

Chapter 2: Anthony the Boxer

In addition to fighting other kids, I got to see a lot of angry kids fighting each other. One of these fights was between James Wilkinson and a boy named Anthony. At that time, James was walking around acting like he was the toughest kid in class. Anthony had just been moved to our class, and he tried to challenge this "tough kid" right away. "Man, you are *not* that tough! Calm down," he said to James one day.

"And just who do you think you are, newbie?" James said back. "I'm a boxer! I know how to use my knuckles, so you better not try that tough stuff on me!" We didn't believe him, but we had to admit that there were a lot of things different about him.

He was way smarter than the rest of us, and from what he told us, he had a good home life. Both of his parents were there, and they treated him kindly and gave him nice clothes to wear. He seemed to just be violent for no reason. That was actually a scary thought! I kept it in my mind that if we ever fought, I would need to find a weapon.

Anyways, Anthony had challenged James, and a fight was bound to happen! And one day, it did. James decided that it was time to defend his honor, and the two of them prepared for battle. True to his word, Anthony was standing like a boxer, and he fought like one too! "I told you I was a boxer!" he shouted. James was surprised, but he still got a couple hits in. Anthony just had the better fighting skills. It made me wonder if he could have handled Mr. Butler!

We later found out that Anthony's anger came from being made fun of for being a "nerd". So, he studied up on boxing and made it his mission to bust up anyone who called him that! Now I don't remember James ever calling him a nerd, but I guess being bumped down to the problem class made Anthony mad at everybody!

Chapter 3: The "Dark Day"

When it comes to angry kids, there was one day I will never forget. I call it the "dark day", even though the sun was bright and shining at the time. Let me tell you what happened.

Me and two other kids were playing outside by the back gate of the house at 507 Mosher Street. As usual, there were no adults watching us. Normally, we didn't care about this, but on that day, I wish we had someone looking after us.

But it was a calm afternoon, and our guard was down. I don't remember the names of the two kids I was with, because I didn't actually know them. I had only asked them over so that I wasn't totally by myself. Either way, it still didn't stop what happened next.

We were just minding our own business, making up our own games, when we looked up and saw a large group of kids that we didn't know walking up to us. I had this really weird feeling inside telling me that something was up, but I ignored it.

Then as they got closer, I saw that they all had weapons in their hands. Come to find out later that this was a "gang", which is a group of people who are up to no good. Apparently, even kids can form gangs. But you should never join them, because they do bad things to people for no good reason.

This gang of kids had finally reached us, and they had us surrounded. "Um, what's going on?" I asked. But there was no response. They just looked at each other, and then they all shouted, "get 'em!" Before we could do anything, it got crazy! Someone with a metal pipe hit me across my arms, which hurt so bad! I was running and hitting blindly, just trying to bust out of that circle and get away. Finally, there was an opening, and I took off like a jet, running and screaming all the way home!

I had been hit in my funny bone, but there was nothing funny about it! I have no idea what happened to the other two kids I was with, but I do know that the next time I was outside and saw a bunch of strange kids walking up, I got outta there lightning quick!

Most kids who join gangs are angry because of situations at home, and they use violence as a way to express themselves and find relief. But this is not the right way. Hurting other people is never the solution when you feel hurt. At that point, you need to find a healthy outlet, like talking to a friend or doing something good for someone else.

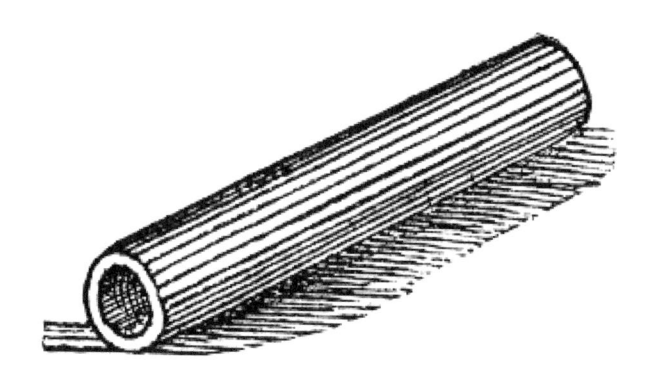

Next Time...

I haven't talked a whole lot about my mother, but stay tuned. She was going through a lot at that time, and I made it my goal to try to protect her as best as I could. That's what I'd like to tell you more about on your next visit. I hope you come back soon! And remember, all of us have a story. Don't be afraid to tell yours!

Questions to Discuss

1. Did David show the proper respect to Mr. Butler?

2. Is it right for a teacher to get physical with a student?

3. How did Anthony feel about being called a nerd?

4. If you get the sense that something bad is about to happen, what should you do?

5. Is it right for kids to form a gang to deal with their anger?

A Young Boy Named David
Book 13
Looking Out For Mom

Written By
David M. Smith

A Young Boy Named David Book 13: Looking Out For Mom

Written By: David M. Smith

Characters

- David – me
- Jonathan – older brother
- Sylvia – mom
- Mr. Hawalfa
- Mr. Charlie
- Mr. Willie

Chapter 1: Mr. Hawalfa

Let's face it; my mom had bad taste in men. My dad was missing, Mr. Sea-Dog was bad, and so was Mr. Hawalfa. I realized later in life that all these bad men over me were causing me to distrust and disrespect authority, which is very dangerous for young ones.

To make matters worse, I was confused because the police never busted down our door and arrested him for the things he was doing to my mom. But let me take a timeout to explain something to you…*the police won't come unless you call them!* So when you see something bad happening, you have to tell someone about it if you want anything to be done about it.

But back to my mom and Mr. Hawalfa. Thankfully, my mom said that enough was enough, and she ended things with him. "I don't want to see you around here anymore. I'm done with you," she let him know. "You know what? Fine! I don't want to be with you anyways. I'm gonna go stay at my brother Joe's house," he replied.

Although my mom was rid of him, it revealed something about her that I didn't realize. My mom came from a family with a lot of brothers and sisters, so she hated being alone. This meant that even if she was with a bad man, she actually felt some safety in that because at least she didn't have to be by herself. When Mr. Hawalfa left, I could tell that she was still in need of someone in her life.

"Mom? Why can't me and Jonathan be enough for you?" I asked her one day. My question had caught her off guard. She pulled me close to her and gave me a big hug. "Oh, my little Monster Mash. You know I love you guys so much. And you make me really happy. It's just...it's just..." Her voice left off, and I didn't question her anymore. I guessed that there must be a special kind of love that only adults could give each other. And based on the kind of guys my mom was around, I knew she was looking for love in all the wrong places. That's when I made it my mission to protect her at all costs!

Chapter 2: Mr. Charlie

It wasn't that long after Mr. Hawalfa that Mr. Charlie came along. He was an older man who lived in a house around the corner. He could get to our house by taking a shortcut through an alley that connected the two buildings. He visited a mechanic shop that was ten feet from our backyard, and a lot of people started going to him to borrow money.

Because of this, he took advantage of a lot of them, and I didn't like him that much. However, since Jonathan was hardly around, he didn't know Mr. Charlie very well. In fact, Mr. Charlie would give him money to do small favors for him. "Hey Jonathan. What do you have there?" "Just some money I got from Mr. Charlie. He wants me to go to the store and buy something for him. He said I could keep the change, too!" "I don't know about him, Jonathan. There's something about him I don't like." "Oh, come on Monster Mash. Don't tell me you're picking on him because he's old and walks with a cane?" "No, it's not like that. I've seen the way he looks at mom. I think he might be spending too much time with her." It turns out that he was trying to get closer ever since Mr. Hawalfa left. Pretty soon, he was her new boyfriend.

I think he became the target for all of my anger that was coming up inside me. I wanted someone to hate, and because he was so close to my mom, I put it all on him. I also didn't like the fact that he had another girlfriend at the place where he lived. Maybe I didn't know a lot about love, but I was smart enough to know that you're only supposed to have one boyfriend or girlfriend at a time!

I don't think my mom knew about the other woman, so to get back at Mr. Charlie, I would steal from him every chance I got. I hoped that this would make him stop coming around as much. Boy, did that backfire! "Sylvia! I think your little monster stole my ten dollars!" he said after checking his pockets. "Monster Mash, is this true?" she asked me. "No mom. I didn't take nothing from him!" I lied. "Besides, why is this man even here? He's old and mean and has another girlfriend!" Wow! Back then I was growing up and beginning to say things to adults that I didn't before. This was a big deal for me to call out a man in his sixties for lying! My mom didn't believe me and thought I was just making it up, but I could tell that from that moment, Mr. Charlie began to see me as an enemy.

Me and him had our screaming battles, and the anger between us was growing. The instant that he gave my mom a hit so hard that it left a mark on her leg, Jonathan joined me in my anger, and the two of us really thought how we could get rid of this guy and stop him from hurting her anymore.

One of our plans was to run up and knock his cane away so he would fall down. Mean, I know, but I was looking out for my mom in any way I knew how! Have you been trying to protect someone? A parent? A friend? Maybe ourselves? If so, then I can relate to what you are feeling. It's best to talk to a trusted adult so you don't feel like you have to protect everyone and everything all by yourself!

One day, I got the chance to teach Mr. Charlie one final lesson for messing with our mother. He was walking alone in the alley behind our house, and I snuck up on him and threw a bottle and a brick at him! This was so wrong of me to do, but at the time it felt so right! But it didn't change anything. He hid in his house for a few days, my mom got really mad at me, and they were still seeing each other. Although I will say that instead of him coming over, she would go outside of the house, so at least I didn't have to see him as much.

Remember how Mr. Charlie had two girlfriends? Well, my mom had two boyfriends. It seems like the adults in the town didn't know much more about love than me! Let me introduce you to Mr. Willie.

Chapter 3: Mr. Willie

Mr. Willie lived by himself, oddly enough on the same block as Mr. Charlie. Mr. Willie didn't really hang out at 507 Mosher Street. So My mom was always at Druid Hills Avenue with either him or Mr. Charlie. My mother at some point put Mr. Charlie to the curb. We were barely spending any time together as a family. Mom started going to Mr. Willie's apartment often. Whenever we wanted to see our mom, we basically had to go over to Mr. Willie's house and shout at his window from the ground.

"Hey, momma! Can you come out?" Mr. Willie popped his head out and yelled, "she'll be right out!" "Why can't we just go up there and get her?" I asked Jonathan. "Mr. Willie says no kids are ever allowed up there," he answered. I wondered why this could be, but we never found out. All we knew was that this new boyfriend was taking up all of our mom' time, and we hated him for it. They would drink from funny bottles together. At least with Mr. Charlie he would come over to our house. Well, at least he would come over before I attacked him in the alley. He actually knew about mom's other boyfriend, so he didn't like Mr. Willie either.

Finally, our mom came out to us, and we were able to tell her what we thought of her staying away from us so much. Jonathan spoke up. "Mom, it's crazy that you're spending all this time away from the house. We don't like it! You need to quit messing around like this and be home with us more." "Excuse me, but when did you guys become parents? You don't tell me what to do!" she said. It was true. We weren't her parents. We were her kids. But that didn't mean that we couldn't try to help her when we saw her doing something bad.

And that's what I want you to know. Some adults might make you feel that you should never speak out to them. But as long as you do it in a nice, respectful way, you should always let an adult know if they're doing something wrong, especially when the things that they do directly affect you.

It was obvious that my mother wasn't able to make good decisions for herself, especially when it came to men. Sure enough, one day she came back from Mr. Willie's house with a mark on her face from where he had hit her, and my brother nearly lost his mind! I had attacked Mr. Charlie, and it seemed like he was about to do the same thing to Mr. Willie. I guess it was a good thing that he never came over to our house! Out of all of mom's boyfriends, he was the smallest one, and grown up or not, you do not want to go up against an angry pre-teen after you hit his mother!

Next Time...

There are a couple people in my life's story I have already mentioned that have more history with me that I can talk to you about. Our lives are shaped by the people we spend the most time with, and based on who those people are, this can be either good or bad. When you come by next time, you'll see how it turned out for me as I tell you more about these familiar faces. And remember that we all have our own story. Don't be afraid to tell yours!

Questions to Discuss

1. If you have a situation where the police need to get involved, what should you do?

2. Why did David's mom not like being alone?

3. Was it right for David to attack Mr. Charlie in the alley?

4. If you see an adult doing something wrong, should you say something?

5. How much time should parents and children spend together?

A Young Boy Named David
Book 14
Familiar Faces

Written By
David M. Smith

A Young Boy Named David Book 14: Familiar Faces

Written By: David M. Smith

Characters

- David – me
- Jonathan – older brother
- Gene
- Mr. Sea-Dog
- Miss Tree
- Mr. Denis
- Miss Pat

Chapter 1: What Was Happening to Jonathan?

As Jonathan grew older, he was acting up more and more. Some of the things he was getting into was taking the childhood right out of him. This meant that me and my brother were not as close as we should have been. He was four years older than me and had a lot more pressure on him. It got to a point where he couldn't handle it anymore, and he started to push me away.

"Hey Jonathan?" I asked him. "What, David?" "Do you think dad will ever come back?" He looked up at me with an annoyed look. "Which one?" I was confused by this. "What do you mean which one?" "You do realize that we don't have the same father, right?" Wow! This was sad information for me! I always thought that we were real brothers, not half-brothers. I found out that Jonathan's dad's name was Gene. We never saw him, and he never saw anything, because he was blind.

I was shocked to hear about him because my mom had given both Jonathan and me her last name. That let me know that she felt the same way about both of our fathers. These were issues that seemed to run in the family. Looking back, we never even learned about my mother's father.

Maybe you have a history in your family of one of the parents not being there. Please know that this doesn't mean that your family did anything wrong or that the pattern has to continue. If someone leaves, that is *their* decision. And let me add that it is a bad decision. And that doesn't mean that you have to turn out that way. If you become a parent at some point, choose to stay and never leave your family. That way you can break the cycle.

Going back to our childhood, my mom was putting too much on my brother's shoulders. She was basically making him raise me, which was way too much for a kid to handle. Neither did Jonathan want it. She was treating him like he was an adult, which was robbing him of his childhood. Maybe that's why Jonathan turned to stealing and robbing everything around him.

I wish I could go back and ask him how he was feeling, what he was going through, and how I could help him. Please ask these questions to anyone in your life that you think is going through a hard time.

That care and attention could help them out in a huge way.

Chapter 2: Mr. Sea-Dog's Good Times

Remember Mr. Sea-Dog? He was one of my mom's earlier boyfriends who got knocked out by my Uncle Bernard. It turns out that after that, Mr. Sea-Dog became a really nice guy! He gladly offered up anything he had to help others, which was a level of sharing that I never saw from anyone else at the house!

His new girlfriend was Miss Tree, and she was also very nice. Surprisingly, her and my mom got along really well! Usually, my mom tried to fight every other woman in sight, so that tells you how special Miss Tree was! They became close friends.

When I look back, I can say that out of all the people my mom dated, Mr. Sea-Dog was my favorite in the end! "Hey! My main man Monster Mash! What's up, youngster?" he said to me as I passed him in the hall. "I'm good, Mr. Sea-Dog!" Since Jonathan was always off running around with his friends, it was nice to have a friendly face at the house. Two friendly faces, counting Miss Tree. He was really nice to her. One time, I saw him take her hand and kiss it gently. "Oh, how sweet of you, dear!" she said with a huge smile on her face. I never saw any woman at the house look that happy.

This put a mark in my mind that being a gentleman was the kind of person I wanted to be when I got older.

      Mr. Sea-Dog was also good at making everybody laugh. He would playfully tease people and dance around whenever music was playing. He definitely brought some good times to the house. But that didn't mean that he didn't have his own problems that had to be dealt with. Nobody is perfect, and we have to be able to handle whatever situations we find ourselves in, whether good or bad.

Chapter 3: Mr. Sea-Dog's Bad Times

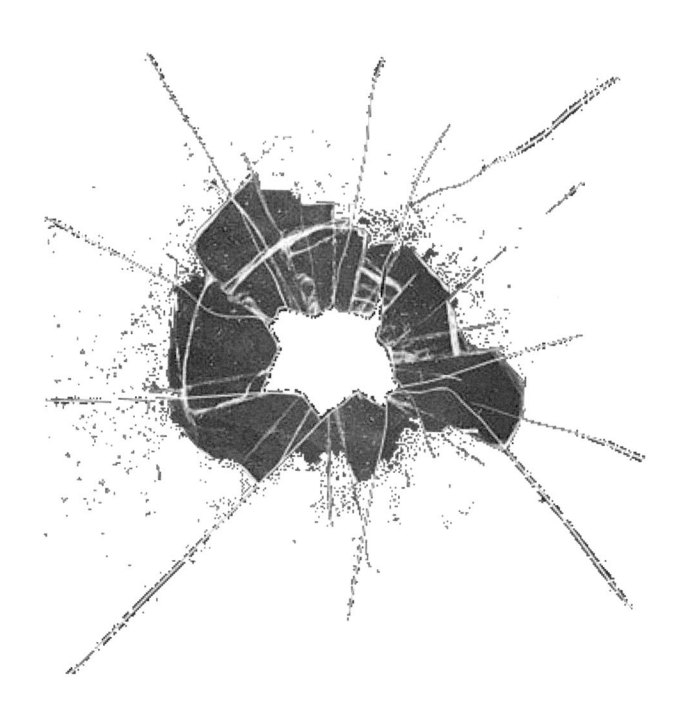

Sadly, Mr. Sea-Dog would sometimes have seizures, which would make his whole body shake and twist uncontrollably at random times. Others at the house had this problem as well, but Mr. Sea-Dog had it the worst.

I called the ones he had "the runners" because when he had them, his head would go back, his eyes would get really focused on something off in the distance, and he would move forward as if someone else was in control of his body. This was really scary for me to see.

One particular day was the scariest time of all! He was in the hallway, standing across from Mr. Denis' room, when a bad case of the runners took hold of him. The next thing I knew, he got that look in his eyes, let his pants drop to his ankles, and started running ahead…straight for the second-floor window! It all happened so fast, and I couldn't believe what happened next, but he ran right through the window! "Help! Help! Mr. Sea-Dog just jumped out of the second-floor window!" I started yelling.

Mr. Denis burst out of his room to find out what was going on. The window was by Miss Precious' room, and so she came out as well. I stayed with her while Mr. Denis ran down the stairs to go outside to check on Mr. Sea-Dog. I feared the worst, but to my surprise, he was still alive! Mr. Sea-Dog was one tough guy to survive! And that wasn't the only time he had a crazy accident.

There was another time when his seizures caused him to have another runner and a bigger fall. This time he landed headfirst on a fence and had to get a glass eye! These accidents moved him to turn to religion in hopes that his faith would protect him from any more danger. And in fact, him and Miss Tree continued to be the nicest people in the whole house. We all benefited from their care and wisdom.

Seeing the way Mr. Sea-Dog used to be and watching him transform into the spiritual man he now was, taught me an important lesson. No matter how life treats you, it's always possible to change and become a good person. I really needed to see this for myself, because at the time I was feeling stuck at 507 Mosher Street with no way out.

But believe me when I say that no matter how bad it gets, if you hold on to hope and find the right examples to follow, there will always be a way out for you!

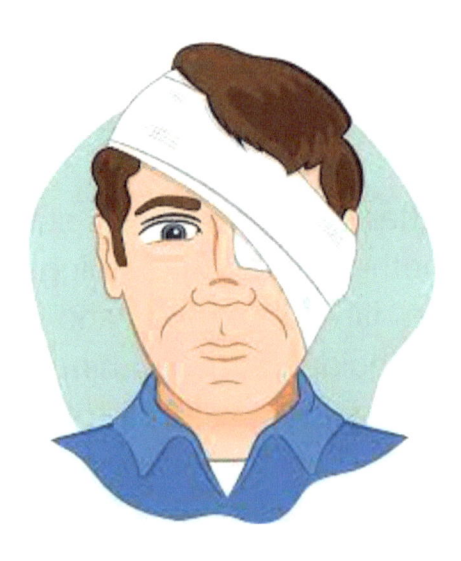

Next Time...

It wasn't until later in life that I applied the lessons I learned from Mr. Sea-Dog's example. Meanwhile, the pain and anger caused from my home life was causing a dark side in me to come out. I'll tell you about how that affected me the next time we get a chance to hang out. Also, remember that we all have our own stories. Don't be afraid to tell yours!

Questions to Discuss

1. Should a mother's children with different fathers act like siblings?

2. What happens when children are asked to grow up too fast?

3. What questions can you ask someone going through a hard time?

4. What changes did Mr. Sea-Dog make?

5. Even if bad things happen in life, can you choose to be a good person?

A Young Boy Named David
Book 15
Going to the Dark Side

Written By

David M. Smith

A Young Boy Named David Book 15: Going to the Dark Side

Written By: David M. Smith

Characters

- David – me
- Willis
- Snooda
- Older Woman
- Jonathan – older brother
- Milton

Chapter 1: "Micey"

Before we lost the Humphreys in an accident, I was getting really close to them. At the same time, my brother met a new family that he was spending time with. I guess he wanted friends that I didn't share with him. Since he had moved on, that left me more time to hang out with Willis, Snooda Humphrey's older nephew. Willis was the thief of the family, and he began to teach me these bad skills.

An important lesson to keep in mind is that who you hang out with can affect how you turn out. When I was spending time with Snooda, I was working hard at the church and doing jobs around the neighborhood to earn my own money. But when I started hanging around Willis, we were going out to the streets and stealing whatever we wanted.

The same thing happened to my brother. Around Willis, he was a thief who liked to sneak around and do things in secret. But after hanging out with Milton and his siblings, who all knew martial arts, Jonathan began fighting more and being more aggressive.

I would have tried to follow Jonathan to Milton's house, but he lived in the same building where my grandmother died, and I didn't like going over there. The painful memories were still fresh in my mind.

One day, while at the Humphrey's house, I made a choice that had a big effect on my life. "Hey David!" Snooda said. "Let's go out and play some games so we can earn some money." Before I could respond, Willis spoke up. "Nah, Micey wants to come with me to steal some stuff, don't you?" Wow! Willis had just given me a new nickname! Now I felt like he was really taking a liking to me. Was this how Jonathan felt? Was the respect and friendship he got from Willis the reason he left me behind? All I know was that I was caught in the middle of my two friends! Would I choose to play harmless games, or turn to crime?

Sadly, that day, I made the wrong choice. "Sorry, Snooda. I'm going with Willis." I had officially gone to the dark side. And I was only headed for more trouble. Oh, and even to this

258

day, I have no idea where the nickname Micey came from, so don't ask!

Chapter 2: Stealing Purses With Willis

I used to always wonder what things my brother and Willis would run off to do. Well, now I was going to find out for myself! My first crime lesson was in stealing purses from older women. "Ok, Micey. Here's how you do it. Watch them as they go into the store. Look at what side of their body they hold their purse, and then run up on them quick when they come out."

To be honest, I didn't feel good about this at first. But if I didn't have Willis, who else would I hang out with? I had ditched Snooda, and my brother had new friends. I didn't want to be alone, so I decided to do whatever Willis told me to.

Have you ever been in that situation before? If so, I understand. The thought of being alone can seem really scary, but you can always find people who do good things to hang out with. They may be at school, or in your neighborhood, and they may not even be your same age. Just keep looking, and you'll find the right ones to be with.

For me, back then, I thought that Willis was all I had, so I agreed to steal my first purse. We were hiding outside of the City Foods supermarket. It was a cold winter day, and we were shivering our little tails off. Finally, someone I thought would be a good target entered the store. "This is your chance, Micey! Be ready," Willis said. I was trying to be, but I was really nervous.

The lady seemed harmless. She was very short, and she was wearing a black hat and a dark coat. I noticed where she put her money, and when she came out and started walking up the alley, I was relieved! Nobody would see us there, so I didn't have to worry about getting caught.

In my excitement, I wasn't doing a good job of sneaking behind her, because she kept looking back and walking faster. Finally, I just ran up and knocked her over, grabbing her purse as she fell. Thankfully, there was plenty of snow on the ground to break her fall, but I accidentally elbowed her in the face when I rushed at her, and her nose started bleeding.

I was about to run off with her money, but then I just had to look at her face, and my heart just crumbled. She looked so sad and hurt, just laying on the ground and crying. Then she said, "please, don't take my money. It's all I have to live on. I'll starve!" Wow! I never thought about how stealing affected the victim. They needed what they had, and what right did I have to take it from them?

A strange feeling took over me, and it caused me to throw her purse back at her and run away as fast as I could. I later learned that feeling was something called guilt. It's something you feel when you know you've done something wrong, and you start to feel bad about it.

If you ever feel guilt like I did, do yourself a favor and listen to it! Now this was my first time trying to steal from someone I didn't know. It turns out the same thing happened to

Willis on his first stealing mission. "It happens. Next time, just don't look them in the face."

I kept stealing with Willis. But what happened next really made me think hard about whether or not this was a good idea.

Chapter 3: Running From the Cops!

Willis decided to upgrade to breaking into cars. This way, we wouldn't have to worry about seeing the people we were stealing from. I guess he thought that we would feel less guilty that way, although we were still doing something wrong.

All I had to do was keep watch, but I was still nervous. We were on a parking deck that was next to a small clinic. "You don't have to look so nervous, Micey. Just whistle if you see someone coming, and then run like the wind!" It seemed easy enough. But just as he was about to bust the window, a police car drove by! "Cops! Run!" I yelled.

We took off running and jumped over the wall to the ground about eight feet below. I landed safely, but just as I was about to get up to start running again…

"OWWWWWW!!!" Willis had jumped after me and landed right on my ankle! It felt like it was broken, and I couldn't move it at all. I looked up, expecting to see Willis offering his hand to help me up. But all I saw was his back as he kept running, leaving me behind.

Wow! I was risking so much to help Willis steal, but the second he might get into trouble, he left me all alone. That was not being a loyal friend, and that hurt me even more than my ankle did. I crawled over to a nearby bush and prayed that the police didn't find me. I waited there for a long time to make sure they were gone. The funny thing was, it turns out that they weren't even looking for us! They had pulled someone over and were just stopping in the parking deck before talking to the driver.

However, after being abandoned by my partner in crime, I was in no laughing mood. I somehow was able to drag myself all the way home. The next time I saw Willis and told him what happened, he just said that he didn't know that I had hurt my ankle. But more than that was hurt. Our friendship had been damaged, and I decided to never steal with Willis again.

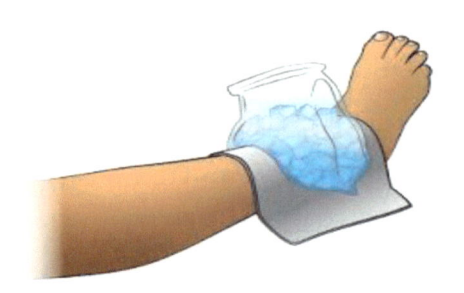

Next Time…

Well, looks like it's time to go back to school. No, not in real life! I'm talking about in my story! The problems I was having outside of school were following me to the classroom, and the fighting and the anger only continued. Next time I'll tell you about how I handled these problems in the wrong way, which will hopefully lead to you handling them in the right way! And remember that we all have our own stories. Don't be afraid to tell yours!

Questions to Discuss

1. What was the difference between Willis and Snooda?

2. Why did David agree to go stealing with Willis?

3. What does it mean to feel guilty?

4. Did Willis really have David's back?

5. Do you think living a life of crime is worth it?

A Young Boy Named David
Book 16
More School Problems

Written By
David M. Smith

A Young Boy Named David Book 16: More School Problems

Written By: David M. Smith

Characters

- David – me
- Mr. German Shepherd
- Willis Humphrey
- Mr. Butler
- James Johnson
- Rhonda
- Timothy

Chapter 1: Lessons From the Street

Instead of getting all my education from school, I was also being taught by the streets. Namely, by Mr. German Shepherd. As a young boy, I had no business being around someone like that. But who else was there taking an interest in me at that point? One lesson he taught me was about not getting cheated out of your money. This man never wanted to pay full price for anything! If we beat him at a game and he was supposed to pay us $10, he would try to get us to accept $5. If we tried to sell him something we found that we knew cost $20, he would talk us down and only want to give us $10. We always had to argue with him to get a fair deal.

This is where Willis stepped in to use his money skills. Since Mr. German Shepherd was his stepfather, he was used to the kind of deals he would have to make with him to not get cheated. The weather was something else we learned to take advantage of.

You see, Baltimore is a very cold city, and in the winters, we normally get a lot of snow. "Hey Micey! Be ready for this weekend," Willis told me. "With all the snow, the police won't be able to walk around the streets, which means we can bust into the corner stores and take whatever we want!"

This time there was over 20 inches of snow! It turns out that kids, teens, and adults all showed up to take part in this super crime. It needs to be said that just because a lot of people are doing something doesn't make it right.

Anyways, many things were stolen that day. And I took my fair share. But even though none of us were caught, I couldn't get rid of the voice in my head saying "David, you have just done a very bad thing."

Chapter 2: Rematch With James Johnson

The crimes I was committing in the streets were seriously affecting my school behavior. I stopped caring about getting in trouble or doing my assignments. All I wanted to do was to get in and out of class so I could go back to running around the streets with Willis. Looking back, the entire time me and my brother knew him, we never saw Willis go to school. "I don't have time for learning," he would say. "Everything I need to know, I can learn on the street."

Really, though, school is the only place you can learn how to be a smart, nice, controlled person with good manners and behavior. I wish I appreciated that fact more in my younger days, but it's not too late for you to stay in school and succeed!

The other kids in my class started to notice that I was changing, and they became really afraid of me. "Man, what is wrong with you?" James Johnson said to me one day. "I don't think you're really as tough as you act." How many times did James have to challenge me before he learned that I was not someone to be messed with?

"Why don't you come over here and say it to my face, James?" I was ready to go crazy on this kid! Mr. Butler stepped in, and as usual, he took us into the bathroom to battle it out. The door was locked, and we were ready to go! Right away, I could tell that he was afraid, and I was able to use this fear to my advantage, The fight was over before it even began!

I ran full force at James and shouted, "I've got you now!" He got so scared that he froze for a second, which was all the time I needed. When I got to him, I put him in a headlock and held on tight until he finally gave up. This was one of the shortest fights I ever had!

When we got back to class, everyone could tell who had won. Rhonda, the only girl in the class, actually started clapping. "Way to go David! I knew you would win." I think she was beginning to like me. But I wasn't looking at girls to fall in love with…at that point, I was only looking for my next fight!

Chapter 3: Battle with Fang Face

One day, another thumb-sucking kid joined the class. His name was Timothy, and he had these weird-looking front teeth that we all made fun of. It was decided that his nickname should be Fang Face. We would make jokes about his teeth almost every day. We could tell that it really bothered him, but that didn't stop us.

I was the one taking the lead in the bullying, and so I was the kid Timothy had the most anger toward. One day, I took it too far. "Hey Fang Face? How do you even eat with those huge chompers of yours?" I said. This got everyone laughing, so I kept going. "I wonder who has bigger front teeth; you or a rabbit!" Timothy was turning bright red, but he was not saying anything. I decided to throw in just one more insult. "I bet your mom has even bigger teeth than you do!"

This was pushing it too far! Timothy got up and shoved me to the ground. Then, he tried to bite my face off! At least, that's what it felt like. I guess I was about to find out what his "fangs" could really do!

We rolled around on the ground for a few minutes. Every time I tried to get him off of me, he just sank his teeth deeper. "Mr. Butler! He's trying to suck David's blood!" one of my classmates shouted. I don't even know which one, because I was so focused on the huge teeth bearing down on me!

I have no idea where Mr. Butler was or what he was doing, but I knew I had to get out of this one on my own. When I saw that my chin was starting to bleed from Timothy's bite, it caused me to fight even harder to push him off of me. He was still holding me down yelling in my face, "I'm tired of you guys making fun of my teeth! Well, do you think they're funny now? ARE THEY FUNNY NOW??" He was shouting at the top of his lungs. Then I realized…if he was yelling, that meant that he wasn't biting me! So the next time he opened his mouth to shout at me, I shoved him back with all my strength.

This surprised him, and he fell backwards. Now I was able to get on top of him, and I hit him in the face about eight times before Mr. Butler finally stepped in and pulled us apart. I had never fought someone that angrily before. In that moment, it was like everything I was going through in my life was coming out in my fists.

This wasn't fair to Timothy. In fact, all he was doing was reacting to the bullying that I had started. He wasn't the reason why my brother abandoned me or that my mom was never around. Timothy wasn't the reason the Humphreys died in a fire or that my dad left me.

Most schools have teachers and counselors in place to help students process these kinds of situations in healthy ways. That's what I should have done; gone to a counselor to get help. And that's what you should do too, if you ever need help dealing with feelings of anger or loss. Don't pick on or beat up some innocent kid. You'll only end up making everyone feel worse that way. I wish I could say that I learned this lesson after my fight with Timothy. But even after moving on to fifth grade, I was still an angry kid, trying to use his fists to make sense of his crazy world. Wow! When would I ever learn my lesson?

Next Time...

Fifth grade only brought more problems and new kids for me to fight with. I hope you don't think that I'm telling you about my battles to brag about how tough I was. No, these fights showed how broken I was on the inside. I want you to see how violence doesn't fill the holes left behind by bad people; it only makes them worse. Stay tuned for my next story, and remember that all of us have our own stories. Don't be afraid to share yours!

Questions to Discuss

1. Was it a good idea for David to hang around adults like Mr. German Shepherd?

2. Since so many people robbed the corner store, was it right to do?

3. Was it right for Willis to drop out of school?

4. How did Timothy feel about being teased because of his teeth?

5. Instead of fighting everyone, who can you go to for help to deal with your emotions?

A Young Boy Named David
Book 17
Fifth Grade Fights

Written By
David M. Smith

A Young Boy Named David Book 17: Fifth Grade Fights

Written By: David M. Smith

Characters

- David – me
- Mr. Butler
- Gary Matthews
- Gary Jones
- Timothy
- David Thompson
- James Johnson
- Mike

Chapter 1: Gary vs. Gary

With all the fighting I was doing, I was surprised that I even made it to the fifth grade! I wonder sometimes if I was just being pushed through so my teachers could get rid of me. But it wasn't like I was the only student causing problems.

I can remember two other kids who fought a lot once we moved up to the next grade. Strangely, they both were named Gary! Gary Matthews (GM) was short, but he had some muscles! And Gary Jones (GJ) had these big glasses that he would wear.

One day, we were walking back to the classroom after lunch time, when the two Gary's started screaming at each other. The issue between them had actually started earlier, at recess. Mr. Butler had been letting us go outside to play kickball, and Gary M was mad when Gary J accidentally ran into him. GM thought that the other Gary had done this on purpose. "Come on, man! Watch where you're going!" I think what made it worse was that the other Gary didn't even try to apologize. "Relax, dude," GJ said. "With those big muscles, you shouldn't have even felt it. Unless they're fake and you're just a big baby!"

You should have seen the look on GM's face! You could tell he didn't like being called a baby. "Oh yeah?" he responded. "Well, with those big glasses, you should have seen where you were going!" They had been going back and forth ever since. It continued into the cafeteria, and now on the way back to class they were still going at it!

By now, we were on the steps leading up to the second floor. Gary Matthews was a few steps higher than Gary Jones. One other thing I should quickly mention was that Gary Jones was a fake tough guy! He tried to act all big and bad, but he wasn't a fighter. That's why we were all surprised when he took on the kid with the biggest muscles! Anyway, none of us were prepared for what happened next.

While we were on the steps, Gary Matthews all of a sudden turned around and punched Gary Jones straight in the face! His glasses went flying off his face, and they must have flipped in the air about three times before they finally hit the ground, next to his knocked-out body!

There were some serious issues going on with all of the kids in Mr. Butler's class. The thing was, we all came from broken families. Most of us didn't have a father. Many adults around us were constantly drinking that bad liquid and being terrible parents. The kids we hung out with were mini criminals with no respect or loyalty. And we felt like no one cared about us. Put a bunch of kids like that in one class, and yeah, you're going to have plenty of fights.

I hope the parents and teachers in your life do all they can to help fix you!

Chapter 2: Timothy vs. David

Remember my fight with Fang Fa...um, I mean, Timothy? Well, the same way I fought two boys named James, he ended up fighting two boys named David. The second fight was with David Thompson. He was a big kid, almost as tall as James Johnson. But with all that size, he wasn't that tough. He would try to avoid fights any way he could. This time, though, he wouldn't be able to get out of a battle that easily. In all the fights he was in, it seems that Timothy was determined to live up to the nickname that we gave him!

On this day, for whatever reason, David Thompson wanted to get some more respect from the class. I guess he had heard about how we were calling him a big softie, and he wanted to win a fight to get us to stop saying that. But he picked the wrong kid to mess with! "Hey, Timothy! I don't like the way you're looking at me. You wanna go?" This was a dumb reason to fight, but David was desperate! "What's a big softie like you gonna do to me?" Timothy replied.

Whenever there was a fight about to happen, there was a serious mood in the room. But this fight would go down as one of the funniest I ever saw! (outside the Remando quarter punch.) The two of them were circling each other, waiting to see who would make the first move. Eventually, David swung his fist high, which allowed Timothy to dodge low. He actually got on all fours like an animal and *chomped down on David's foot!* It was the craziest thing!

And to make matters worse, Timothy was growling and drooling and had a crazy look in his eyes. David was terrified, but the rest of us were busting out laughing!

Finally, David shook his shoe off of his foot, and the fight was basically over. We were all on the ground, laughing our heads off, while Timothy was running around with David's shoe, jumping up and down like he had won a prize.

But really, fighting is no laughing matter. When kids are at the point where they feel like they have to fight for their honor, there needs to be help from adults to make sure that each child feels loved and valued in healthy ways. Fighting is not fun…fighting is fear. Don't be afraid to open up and get the help you need to calm down.

Chapter 3: Mike vs. James

Another new kid in our fifth-grade class was named Mike. Little Mike we called him. He was a short kid who walked funny and wore these really thick glasses. We would call them "coke bottles", and he didn't like that teasing very much.

Because of this, he started acting like he was gonna hit someone. Turns out, that person was going to be James Johnson. This was another funny match up, because James was so much taller than little Mike!

I don't even remember what started the fight, but what I saw will never be forgotten. Mike stood up and ran full speed at James. That's when James lifted his leg, brought it back, and kicked Mike right in the chest! "Don't come at me like that, little boy!" James shouted out. James' feet look like size ten's men's. Mike had tried to hold onto James' big foot, but he still went flying back. It was like James had kicked a football!

Mike was on the ground crying, while James was celebrating winning his first fight in Mr. Butler's class. Surprisingly, even after losing, Mike still had something to say. He stood up and looked at all of us and said, "you guys are mean to me for no reason. Why don't you think about what it means when you call me a midget? It hurts my feelings! And I don't care who it is. If anyone else calls me that, I'll run at you too. I will not back down. Ever!"

Wow! Even though little Mike had lost this fight, he won our respect. We could see that he was not gonna take any more insults! Honestly, we should respect everyone like that. After all, the golden rule is to treat others the way you want to be treated. So if you don't want to be called names, don't do it to anyone else!

Next Time…

Back at home, there were new people moving in. They were interesting, to say the least! When we get more time to talk, I'll let you know what they were like and how I was affected by them. Don't forget that we all have our own stories to tell. So remember to share yours!

Questions to Discuss

1. Should you make fun of kids that wear glasses?

2. Why did the kids in David's class fight each other so much?

3. Are fights something you should laugh at?

4. How did Mike stand up for himself after his fight?
5. What is the golden rule?

A Young Boy Named David
Book 18
New People Moved In

Written By
David M. Smith

A Young Boy Named David Book 18: New People Moved In

Written By: David M. Smith

Characters

- David – me
- Mr. Jessie
- Miss Iris
- Sylvia – mom
- Miss Beatty
- Mr. Muscles

Chapter 1: Mr. Jessie & Miss Iris

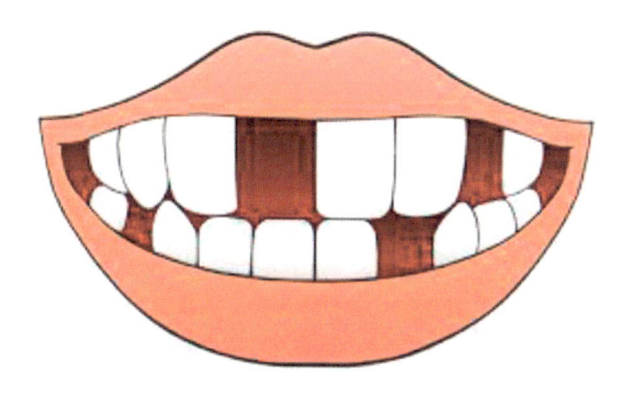

While I was in fifth grade, a very strange couple moved in. Their names were Mr. Jessie and Miss Iris. No one knew where they came from; one day, they were just there at the house.

Miss Iris was a tall woman, while Mr. Jessie was a short man. I guess he tried to make up for his lack of height with his mouth. He was the loudest person in the whole house! The joke was, between Miss Iris' height and Mr. Jessie's voice, you could see or hear them coming from miles away!

One day he opened his window and shouted full blast, "GOOD MORNING MOSHER STREET!" He was like an alarm clock for the whole house that morning. Both he and Miss Iris were missing teeth. She would always try to kiss me on the cheek, and that got on my nerves! The reason for them losing their teeth was probably because they drank that bad liquid all day. It also gave her bad breath and made her suffer from seizures, like the ones Mr. Sea-Dog had.

Sad to say, but my mom would begin to have seizures too. I hated to see her like that, but at least I had an idea of what to do based on how I saw Mr. Jessie take care of Miss Iris. For example, one day I was walking past their small room, and the door happened to be open. I took a peek inside and saw Miss Iris shaking on the floor, in the middle of a seizure. I also saw Mr. Jessie making sure that her tongue was out of her mouth and that he placed a spoon there. Without thinking, I openly said, "what are you doing that for?" Now he knew that I was watching him.

Without overreacting, he told me why. "I'm making sure that she doesn't swallow her tongue and choke." I had never thought about that before. But now, every time my mom had a seizure, I made sure that her tongue was out of her mouth and a spoon was placed there. Looking back now, I should have called 9-1-1. They are the ones trained to take care of people in that condition.

There's something else I learned from Mr. Jessie and Miss Iris, and that was to stay far away from that bad liquid! If it was going to make me look, smell, and act like that, I didn't want anything to do with it!

307

Chapter 2: Miss Beatty

Miss Iris and Mr. Jessie didn't last as a couple. That's when he began seeing Miss Beatty. Boy, was she a mean lady! And not only that, but she didn't seem to be right in the head. She would do some of the craziest things.

For example, she would steal your food and eat it, but then lie to your face and say she didn't do it! One day, I overheard her and Mr. Jessie arguing about this. "I'm telling you, I know you ate my hamburger!" Mr. Jessie shouted at her. She screamed back, "I'm telling you, I did not!" "You had to, because there's no one else in this room!" Right at that moment, Miss Beatty looked out of the slightly cracked door and saw me walking by. She got an evil grin on her face, and I could tell what was coming next.

She pointed at me and said, "it was him! David stole your hamburger!" I was shocked! I had never even been in that room the entire time I lived at 507 Mosher Street! Thankfully, Mr. Jessie didn't believe her. But these were the kind of lies she would tell all the time. It was almost like lying was a disease, and she couldn't help herself.

Miss Beatty didn't respect men at all, and Mr. Jessie was just her next victim. She shouted at him, lied to him, stole from him, and ultimately, she caused a situation that caused him damage that he couldn't recover from. Aside from messing with Mr. Jessie, Miss Beatty also had some fights with my mom. Looking back, I must have gotten my skills and desire for fighting from my mother!

She didn't like any women at the house, but she especially disliked Miss Beatty. "You are an evil woman!" she said one time while they were fighting. "Yes, and you forgot crazy!" Miss Beatty responded. She had another evil grin on her face, showing off her lack of teeth and her I-don't-care-about-anything attitude.

Be careful around people who do bad things and are actually proud of it! You can't trust them, and you might end up getting seriously hurt, or worse…like poor Mr. Jessie. But before we end this story, there's one more person I need to tell you about.

Chapter 3: A Man Named Muscles

Mr. Muscles moved into the house shortly after being let out of prison. Who knows what he was in jail for or how he came to hear about our house? All I knew was that he reminded me of Gary Matthews from my class: he was short, but his body was stacked with muscles. It was obvious how he got his nickname!

Mr. Muscles had the kind of personality of always wanting to be in control. To do this, he would say or do whatever it took to get close to people who he thought could help him. I'm sure he learned this while he was behind bars. He carried this way to our house, and it caused a lot of trouble!

Aside from trying to control people, Mr. Muscles was not afraid to use violence to get his way. Just like how Miss Beatty got in between the relationship of Mr. Jessie and Miss Iris, it seems that Mr. Muscles was about to do the same thing to Mr. Jessie and Miss Beatty. He pretended to be friends with Mr. Jessie, but it was all fake.

He also tried to get close to just about every woman in the house, including my mother! But as bad and rude as he was, the only woman who liked him at all was Miss Beatty. I guess it's true what they say, that the kind of people you attract to your life are the ones who are like yourself. Anyways, because she wanted to be with Mr. Muscles, Miss Beatty was being meaner than usual to Mr. Jessie.

"I hate being around you! You know what? It's over between us!" she yelled at Mr. Jessie one night. It was late, and their argument was waking up the entire house. "Let me guess," he shouted back. "You're gonna go be with that fool Muscles, huh? I already know you guys are getting close. If only he was here right now! I would…" "You would what?" Oops! Mr. Muscles had entered the room, and with all the arguing, Mr. Jessie hadn't noticed.

The sounds we next heard coming out of that room were loud and terrifying. You could tell that things were being broken, curse words were being said, and a fight was taking place. But unlike my fights at school, only one person would walk away…and it turns out that Mr. Jessie was no match for Mr. Muscles. Even though he had been released from prison, he still acted like a criminal, and what he did to Mr. Jessie that night put him right back in jail. This time, he wouldn't be coming out.

Friends, when I say that you have to be careful who you choose to hang out with, it's not just true for when you are younger. Even as you grow up, you need to keep good company. Because if you choose the wrong friends, then like Mr. Jessie, it could end up being the last thing you ever do.

I don't mean to scare you! But I know that some of you have seen and heard terrible things, even at such a young age. Rather than let those things scare you, it's better to find out what you can learn from them. That way, you can grow into a strong person who won't make those same mistakes in life.

Next Time…

Life was moving at a fast pace for me, and before I knew it, I was headed to middle school! A whole new world of people and experiences was waiting for me, and I can't wait to tell you what happened next to this young boy named David! Remember, we all have our own stories. Don't be afraid to share yours!

Questions to Discuss

1. What should you do if someone you know is having a seizure?

2. Do you think it's ok to tell lies like Miss Beatty?

3. Why do you think it's important to be honest in your relationships?

4. Is it good to pretend to be someone's friend just to get something?

5. What scary things have you been through? How did it make you feel?

A Young Boy Named David
Book 19
Graduating to Middle School

Written By
David M. Smith

A Young Boy Named David Book 19: Graduating to Middle School

Written By: David M. Smith

Characters

- David – me
- Sylvie – my mom
- Miss Garner
- Nichole – my crush
- "Stink" Ellington – my cousin
- Mr. Blato

Chapter 1: Sixth Grade

Can you believe it? I had finally made it to the sixth grade. Wow! I couldn't wait to meet my new teacher on the first day. "Hello class. My name is Miss Garner. I'm looking forward to a great year with you all." I can tell you right now: Miss Garner was one of the best teachers I ever had. You could tell that she really wanted to help her students. She was gentle, but she also didn't mess around when it came to keeping us in line.

"David? Can you stay after class so we could talk for a bit?" Uh-oh. How was I already in trouble on the first day? I hadn't done anything! Actually, I was wrong about that. "David, it's nice to meet you in person after all I've heard about you. I just wanted to let you know that all of your fighting will not be accepted in my class. Are we clear?" Yes, ma'am," I said in a quiet voice.

At first, I was embarrassed about her calling me out like this, but it turns out she was really worried about my behavior and wanted me to do well. And I felt it every day by the way she treated me. "Good morning, David! How are you feeling today?" "I'm fine Miss Garner." Then she would flash a bright smile in my direction. It had been a long time since anyone had made me feel like they truly cared about me. That's why Miss Garner will always have a special place in my heart.

Miss Garner's class had twice as many students as Mr. Butler's class, so every time I walked in her classroom, I would get really scared and nervous. It turns out I was afraid of being around so many kids at the same time. It was probably all this fear that took away all the energy I had been using to fight people!

I can still remember some of the kids who were in that class. It was so big that we actually had three girls named Nichole! I teased one of them for her freckles, another one I was friends with, and I had a huge crush on the third one! However, she did not like me back at all. "Umm…hey Nichole. You, uh, look nice today," I mustered up the courage to say to her one day. She took one look my way and said "Ew! Get your smelly self away from me. And why don't you change your clothes for once? You definitely need a fashion upgrade."

Oh man! That one hurt. She really didn't have to be that mean to me, but I guess it wouldn't have hurt me to take a few more baths. Although, getting bathroom time at my house was next to impossible!

Speaking of stinky smells, "Stink" was our nickname for a kid named Ellsworth. It turns out he was my Aunt Gloria's son. It was actually cool to have a family member in the class with me. He was able to introduce me to some of the other boys he was cool with. "Hey David," Stink said. "Meet some of my other friends. That's Glen. Better have some quarters on hand when you're around him. He loves to bet on playground games! Oh, and there's James Ellis. We call him Bubbles, cus he'll blow right by you on the basketball court!"

There were some other boys in the class I was cool with, like Bobby and James, who both had huge heads! There was also Little Frank (whose dad was a mechanic), Donte, James, and Russell. We were all just a bunch of kids trying to find our way in a big, scary city. We liked to hang out together while were in class, but the boys knew that as soon as that bell rang, I was outta there, off to hang out in the streets, the only real home I knew.

Chapter 2: Leaving Mosher Street?

Life at the house at 507 Mosher Street was a daily battle to stay alive. The adults were too busy drinking to look after me, and they also did nothing to take care of keeping the home neat and clean. Many people living there were having bad accidents, which might be why new people slowly stopped wanting to move in.

At this time, there was good news and bad news. The good news was that my mom finally seemed to be getting control over her problem with the bad liquid. "Hey mom. I'm really proud of you!" I said to her one day, giving her a big hug. "And what would that be for, my little Monster Mash?" Mom, it's *Micey* now," I reminded her. She just laughed and rolled her eyes. "Anyways," I continued, "it's been three days since I've seen you have your last drink!" She gently smiled at me and softly said, "yes, I'm working on it baby. I'm working on it."

The bad news at this time was a rumor going around that Mr. Blato, the homeowner, was thinking about selling the property at 507 Mosher Street. "You people just aren't making me enough money on your rent. Thanks to all of your issues, the building is literally falling apart, and I've had several of you get badly hurt, making people think this place is cursed!

I'm getting rid of this property soon, so you all had better start looking for a new place to live!"

Honestly, no one really seemed to care that much. We just had to get our minds wrapped around going to a new place. "Mom," I asked. "What are we gonna do? Where are we gonna stay?" I can't say that I loved 507 that much, but it was scary thinking about not knowing what was going to happen next. Eventually everything worked out. My mom had two sisters, Gloria and Cynthia, who moved out of their apartment at 2202 Tioga Parkway and let us move in there.

But before that happened, this sudden change that was coming had me really distracted from my schoolwork. I couldn't focus in class, and I couldn't even remember what we were learning each day. The only place where I felt like I fit in was on the streets. If you've ever failed a class because of problems and changes at home, then I hope you find a teacher like Miss Garner…or that they find you!

She was a kind and loving teacher who always asked about how I was doing. To be honest, I didn't open up to her like I should have. So please learn from me. If a nice teacher makes it known that they really care about you and want you to be ok, respond to them. They just might be the light you need to make it out of the darkness surrounding you.

Chapter 3: Seventh Grade

Next up in my school journey was seventh grade. I honestly have no idea how I was graduating each year. But somehow, I kept moving on up. I remember being in the gym for our graduation ceremony, and the words of that famous Diana Ross song started echoing out: *"I believe the children are our future..."* I remember these words giving me hope. Maybe things would start getting better for me. I glanced over and saw my crush, Nichole. I waved at her, but she just plugged up her nose and looked away.

That was it. I had to get some new clothes! But who would buy them for me? Up to that point, I don't remember anyone giving me new clothes. My mom was doing better with her health, and she was spending more time talking with her brothers and sisters who lived nearby, but they didn't send me clothes either. Thankfully, my struggles in this area were soon to be over. But for now, it was a miracle that I was able to find clothes to wear each day!

I can remember daydreaming about what it would be like to enter high school one day soon. "You have nothing to worry about, David," Miss Garner tried to reassure me. "Booker T. Washington High

Scholl will be great! Everyone in the city goes there. That's actually where I went to high school!" Her words were meant to encourage me, but all I could think about was being around kids two to three years older than me, and what that would be like.

I also felt like I wasn't ready for high school. My grades weren't great, I didn't do well in crowds, and I had spent so much time fighting kids when I was younger that I didn't feel like I knew enough to be a high school kid.

I began to close myself off from the other kids. They didn't bother me, and I didn't bother them. Instead, I chose to make my relationships and friendships with people I met in my adventures on the streets. But let me tell you…this got me into situations that I hope will never, ever happen to you. The best advice I can give is to stay in school and surround yourself with good and kind kids and teachers. And if you already know some like that, give them a big hug and thank them for being so nice!

Next Time...

You know, you are really a great friend! I wish I could spend all day talking with you and sharing my stories. I've got to go, but the next time we hang out, I've got some really important things to talk to you about. Stay tuned until then! And remember that all of us have our own stories, Don't be afraid to share yours!

Questions to Discuss

1. How do you feel about one day moving on to middle school, and then high school?

2. Dou you find it hard to make new friends when starting a new grade?

3. How did Miss Garner show that she really cared about David?

4. Do you feel embarrassed when your parents can't buy you new clothes?

5. Is it better to make friends with kids at school or strangers on the streets?

A Young Boy Named David
Book 20
Stop Right There!

Written By
David M. Smith

A Young Boy Named David Book 20: Stop Right There!

Written By: David M. Smith

Characters

- David – me
- Willis
- The bad man

Chapter 1: Following After Willis

You really have to be careful who you hang out with. Just like a sponge, you'll end up soaking up whatever things they do...good or bad. That's what happened when I started hanging around Willis more. He already had me running around the streets, stealing things and breaking the law. Now, he had me ditching school to hang out in the streets all day.

That's why I'm so surprised that I ever made it to the next grade. I was hardly ever in class and can barely remember what I was supposed to learn. This was sad. In fact, because I wasn't being taught by teachers, I got my lessons from people in the street. And let me tell you, this was dangerous!

Have you ever heard of a good conscious? Or common sense? These things help you to figure out what is right and wrong, what is good and bad. Well, the people I was spending my time with didn't have these things. They made their own dumb rules, and I followed along with them.

I began to go wherever Willis went and to do whatever Willis did. I should have been smart enough to make my own decisions, but because I wasn't training that part of my brain, it was like it wasn't even there.

Please don't be like me! Find friends who will help you make good choices and stay safe. If you do that, then the situation that Willis was about to lead me into might never happen to you at all.

Chapter 2: The Grey Church

It's possible to become very confused by the things that happen to you. Sometimes, you can meet bad people in a place that's supposed to be good. This happened to me at the church across the street from Snooda and Mr. German Shepherd.

But at this point in my life, I was hanging out more with Willis, getting into things that we had no business getting into. One day, he approached me with a new "deal" he wanted me to help him with. "What's up Willis? You look like you have something big to tell me."

"You bet Micey," he replied. "The pastor at the church wants to cut us in on a special project." I thought this was strange, because Willis and his family didn't go to church much. Actually, neither did anyone else I knew of at that time. I guess everyone was too busy drinking, partying, and running the street to slow down and make time for church on Sundays. So I was really interested in what the pastor would want from two rough kids like me and Willis.

"What kind of project? Is it for the church? Man, you know I don't have good church clothes." "No

Micey, it's not like that. Look, I'm not supposed to tell you anything until we have our secret meeting, but he wants us to sell some stuff for him to a few of the kids we know. He'll pay us really well." Hmm. That was another detail that didn't seem right. Why couldn't the pastor sell whatever it was to the kids himself. Shouldn't he just go to their parents? And what was this about some secret meeting?

None of this was making much sense. But the sad thing was, I ignored all of these warning signs simply because I wanted to do whatever Willis was doing, whether it was good or bad. If he said bad words, I did it. If he stole purses and broke into cars, I did it. So if he was going to start selling random stuff for the pastor, I was going to do it too.

"You can count me in Willis. When and where is this meeting supposed to happen?" I asked. "I'm glad you're in," he said. "The pastor told me to head to the church as soon as you said yes. Let's head over there now!" This put my mind at ease. If we were meeting at a church, I thought, then at least nothing bad would happen. Little did I know that the real truth about my thinking was about to hit me like a brick wall…and boy, those bricks hit HAAAAAARRRRRDDDDD!!!!

We made our way to the grey church. I had never been to it before. But it was a big church, and there were lots of rooms. On top of that, the pastor was a stranger to me too. But all my faith and trust was in Willis. This was just a chance to make some extra money. Hey, maybe I'd be able to afford some new clothes to impress Nichole!

But this thought was pushed back by a weird feeling. First, the pastor gave me a really strange look when he first saw me. I got the feeling that he was looking at me in a way that was wrong, but because I had never had that happen before, I moved past it. But then I thought it was weird that we seemed to be the only people there that day. The lights were turned really low, and we kept going to rooms that took us further and further into the building.

"Willis," I whispered. "Are you sure this is right? Don't you feel weird?" "Nah, Micey," he replied. "I've seen tons of teenagers walk in with the pastor and leave with money. Just relax and be cool." Well, now I couldn't relax. What was a pastor doing sneaking children into deep dark rooms to get them to sell stuff to other kids? It sounded like trap, but I just didn't know what it could possibly be a trap for. My little mind just didn't know of such things back then.

We finally got to a point where the pastor stopped, turned around, and started chit chatting with us. The weird thing was, the whole time, his hands were slowly reaching out towards us, and I didn't know why.

At this point, let me stop and explain something very important to you. Everyone likes to get hugs, hi-fives, handshakes, fist bumps, and similar things. And if you're playing tag, you might tap someone's shoulder or back or head. You may even hold hands with people you like and are close to. These are all fine things to do. But you have parts of your body that no one, and I mean NO ONE, should ever, ever touch. Not even your best friend, a family member, or even your parents.

343

These are your No!No! zones. That's because it's a big no-no if anyone even gets close to them. The thing is, even if you don't know where they are, your body is designed to let you know when someone is getting too close to them. You'll get this really weird feeling, like something is wrong. Your face might turn red, you'll want to cry, or you'll feel really embarrassed.

In fact, you might feel so embarrassed that you don't want to tell anyone that it happened. If it was a stranger that badly touched you, you might feel like no one will believe you since you don't know their name or who they are. But worse, if you *do* know the person, you may be confused as to why they would do this to you, they may tell you to keep it "just our little secret", or you may have liked that person and trusted them, and you don't want to get them in trouble. Or that person may have told you that they would hurt you if you ever told what they did.

I know it is really scary for you if that ever were to happen. In fact, I pray that it doesn't. But if someone makes you feel afraid, if someone makes you feel this way, you have to tell someone. And even if you know their name, you tell on them. Don't be ashamed. You need to tell someone. You *don't* have to take this kind of torture. And if they ask, tell them you're not coming over. Just stay away! If someone's by your No!No! zone, you run away and let them know: YOU'RE GONNA TELL SOMEONE!

Chapter 3: Blame the Person, Not the Place

Sadly, on that day when me and Willis met with the pastor at the church, he touched our No!No! zones. It was a strange feeling that I'll never forget. There were so many things going through my mind, it took me a long time to process everything. I suddenly realized that there was never any money to be made or anything to sell. This was a trap, just like I thought it was. A trap to get young boys to…well, you know what he did. The same thing could happen to girls too. And the bad person that touches you could be a man or a woman.

Who knows if this had happened to Willis before. But let me tell you something. Everyone will react to getting their No!No! zone touched in different ways. Some will immediately run away, screaming and shouting. Others will let it happen, probably because they didn't see it coming and are in shock. But after it happens, they come to their senses and let someone know what happened. For some, though, their way of dealing like it is pretending that it never happened, or worse, that it's not wrong. Either way, you could tell that neither of us were comfortable with what was happening.

You would think that after what happened to me, I would never want to set foot in a church again. But that wasn't the case. I eventually came to learn that it wasn't the church that was bad. Also, that man wasn't bad because he was a pastor. That specific man was bad, and that was it. And that's a lesson I want you to learn. If you were hurt by a person with a certain title, not everyone with that same title will be bad. And if that bad touching happened in a certain place, you aren't in danger every time you go to a similar place. You just have to be on the lookout for warning signs.

Like for me, there were plenty of signs to let me know that something bad was about to happen. For example, Willis asked to go to a place that he didn't normally go to meet with a person I had never met before in a dark room at a time that didn't make any sense to sell things I knew nothing about to kids, but not their parents. Wow! Looking back, it was so obvious that this was a trap!

Simply put, if your brain or body is telling you that something doesn't seem or feel right, listen! That's the best way to keep yourself safe. Next to that, if you think someone is about to touch you in a weird way, then *before* they do it, put your hand up and tell them to stop right there! And then, of course...you have to tell someone!

Thankfully for me, this was the one and only time that someone touched me in my No!No! zone. Who knows, maybe these kinds of things happened to my brother when he wasn't at the house. I know that some of you who are reading this right now have had this happen to you. If that's true for you, then I am so, so sorry. You didn't do anything wrong. Somebody did something wrong to you. I hope that by now you have told a good adult what happened. If you've been keeping it a secret...now is the time to let someone know. You don't have to keep running into that brick wall. Let someone you love and trust help you to break it down! I love you, my little friend! Please feel better!!

Next Time...

Wow! That was intense! But it felt good to tell you about that part of my life. Isn't it a good feeling to talk to a friend and get that huge weight off your shoulders? So far, it seems like my life has been one bad thing after another. But next time, I can't wait to tell you about the absolute best thing that ever happened to me! I'm talking about real hope, true love, a good environment, and more! Please come back so I can share the best part of my story with you! And remember that all of us have a story to tell. Don't be afraid to tell yours!

Questions to Discuss

(You might want to go over some of these questions privately with a teacher, parent, or counselor)

1. Is it ok for anyone to touch your No!No! zones?

2. What signs did you notice that told you David was walking into a trap?

3. Was it right for David to follow Willis and ignore all the warning signs?

4. Should you blame the place where something bad happens?

5. If you were hurt by someone with a specific title, is everyone with that same title bad?

6. What should you say and do if someone tries to touch you badly?

7. Should you feel embarrassed to speak up if you ever get touched in a bad way?

8. Who can you tell if this happens?

A Young Boy Named David
Book 21
A Mother to Love Me

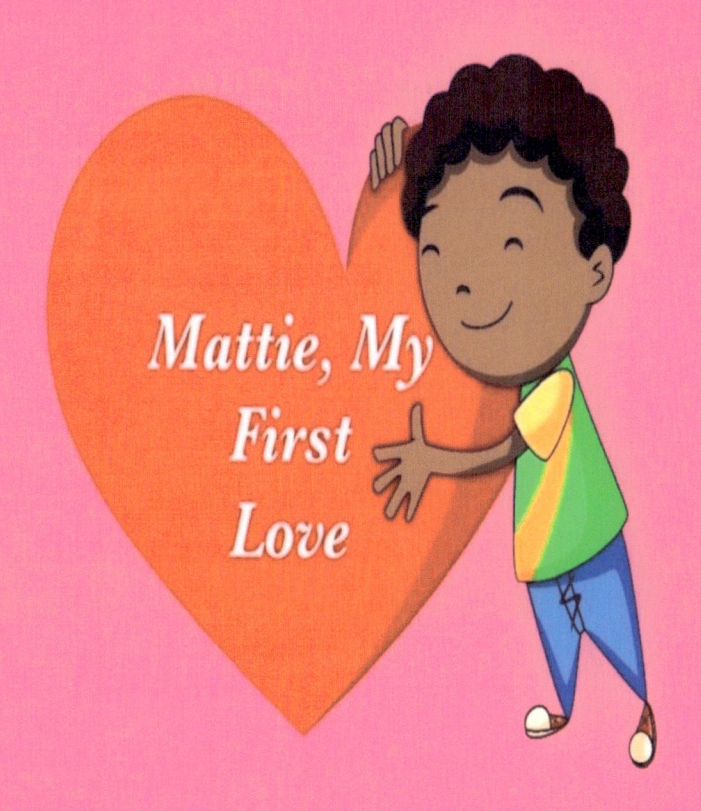

Mattie, My First Love

Written By
David M. Smith

A Young Boy Named David Book 21: A Mother to Love Me

Written By: David M. Smith

Characters

- David – me
- Mack – my dad
- Mattie
- Sylvie – my mom
- Aunt Gloria
- Aunt Cynthia

Chapter 1: More of My Mom's Family

At this point in my life, I was beginning to spend more time around my mom's family. On the weekends, some of my mom's siblings would come over to hang out. I remember them staying up all night to play cards and listen to music. Those games must have been intense, because they always ended in yelling and arguing.

My mom had two sisters, Gloria and Cynthia, that she didn't really like too much. However, Aunt Gloria and Aunt Cynthia were like best friends! If you saw one of them, then the other one was bound to be nearby.

It turns out that my mom didn't like them because they were always trying to convince her to stop drinking the bad liquid so she could take better care of me and Jonathan. Because she didn't want to change her ways just yet, this made her mad, but it made me really like them. It showed that at least I had some family members who cared about how I was doing.

My two aunts lived a bit further away from us in a neighborhood that was less dangerous than where Mosher Street was, and the main focus of their lives was totally different. They got away from the games and the parties and began to get more serious. They shared a small apartment together while Aunt Cynthia went to college to learn about computers.

Both of them were doing really good, and they continued to show love to us. When they moved out of 2202 Tioga Parkway, they let me, my mom, and Jonathan stay there. This was perfect timing, because we had just found out that Mr. Blato was planning to sell the property at 507 Mosher Street.

I thank these two women for showing me love, trying to help my mom, and even showing me a couple things about computers. But the family I was about to find would help me out more than I ever thought was even possible!

Chapter 2: Introduction to My Father

There were a lot of changes happening in my life at this time. But one of the biggest ones was when I actually got to spend some time staying with my father. I must say, it was a weird feeling. I had spent so many years of my life without him, wondering where he was. I'm not even really sure why all of a sudden I was around him more.

It was a really new situation. I got to see a side of my father that I had never seen before. One thing I learned was that my father was a hard worker. He drank like my mom did, but it never caused him to miss a single day of work. Somehow, he was very popular and was like the king of his block! He lived in the Poplar Grove neighborhood in North Avenue, and everyone seemed to like him.

My father's name was Mack, and I would always look forward to the weekends when I would head over to his house on my pink skateboard. "Seriously David?" my brother asked. "You're riding a *pink* skateboard?" "Yeah, so what?" I responded. "It gets me where I need to go!" I don't know why everyone made a big deal about colors. Thankfully, no one else teased me about this. Besides, I had bigger things on my mind. I was headed to Poplar Grove!

With my brother basically abandoning me and not wanting to be around me anymore (except to make fun of my skateboard, apparently), I felt like my father was now the only male family member I had that somewhat was interested in me. I looked forward to my visits with him.

"Hey you guys. I want you to meet my son, David," he would say as he introduced me to his friends. I liked this at first. But as time went on, I realized that it would have been better if he treated me like a son instead of just saying it. I could tell that he had a lot of friends, people respected him, and he had a good job working with cement. So I couldn't figure out what was stopping him from being there for me as a father.

"Dad?" I asked him one day. "What's up, little man?" "Do you make a lot of money at your job?" "You bet! I'm bringing in $500 a week!" "And it seems like most of the people in the neighborhood think you're a pretty good guy." "Oh yeah, I'm pretty much cool with everyone here. I respect them and they respect me." Now my eyes were tearing up, but I tried not to let him see. I had one more question for him. "So overall, would you say you are happy in life right now?"

This was his chance. I wanted him to look at me and say that no, he wishes he could have been there for me instead of leaving, that he thinks about what he did to me every day and wants to be a better dad to me now to make up for it. Instead, without even stopping to think about it, he said, "yeah, I'd say life is pretty good right now!"

Those words broke my heart and filled me with the worst anger and rage I had ever felt up to that point. When a parent leaves, you spend all day thinking of possible reasons why they did it, trying to make sense of everything. So when you find out that they left because they simply didn't care…talk about hitting a brick wall.

I would have become a lost cause at that point. But there was an angel in my life that I was about to meet. My dad had a girlfriend named Mattie, and she proved to be the greatest force of love and motherly care that ever came my way during my childhood. By the way she treated me, she literally saved my life.

As for you, yes, it's true that one of your parents may have left. But stay on the lookout for the man or woman that is guaranteed to fill that place for you. There is someone out there who will really love and care about you. Because every little heart, no matter how damaged, deserves to have that kind of person in their life!

Chapter 3: Mattie, My First Love

How do I even begin to describe what Mattie meant to me? She may have been my father's girlfriend, but she was the love of my life! She did more things for me than my own mother did, and she definitely gave me the feeling of being my mom. She didn't have children of her own, and she seemed glad to take me on as one of her kids.

My dad may have told people that I was his son, but Mattie actually treated me like it! "Ooh, little David! I'm so glad to see you this weekend," she said to me one day when I came over. "I decided to cook you a big breakfast! There are eggs, pancakes, hash browns, and orange juice, all on the table for you. I'll sit next to you, and we can talk about your week."

Wow! My mouth dropped open so wide that you could drive a city bus through it! I had never in my life had a meal cooked just for me, with the chance to sit and talk with someone who was interested about what was happening with me! This showed me of what it really meant to have a normal family life. Eating together, talking together, laughing together…it was all so nice!

It turns out Mattie was the kindest person in the whole neighborhood! She would also cook for some of the other kids on the block. To be honest, this made me a little jealous at first. I wanted Mattie all to myself! But when you have as much love as she did, it makes sense that she gave it out to as many people as she could. But she did show me special attention that no one else got. In fact, if you asked anybody in the neighborhood who Mattie's son was, they would say, "her son is that young boy named David!"

Another memory I have is her giving me my first proper bath. "Oh, Daviiiid!" she sung out to me one afternoon when I was over. "It's time that I give you a proper bath!" "Aw, no! I'm too old for you to be bathing me. I'm not a baby!" I pushed back. But secretly, I was looking forward to being babied.

She turned on the warm water, filled the tub with bubbles, and even put some toys in there for me to play with. Then she left me to myself while she went around the house cooking, cleaning, and even singing. That moment in time made me feel so much joy and warmth in my heart. I finally realized why I was so angry all of the time. I was mad and fighting because I didn't have the loving environment that I know I needed. But now, I finally had it!

I can't remember my own mother ever cooking me a meal, giving me a bath, or buying me new clothes. Mattie did all of those things for me, and she did the with love. I sat in the tub thinking about all these things. When she came back in to put more suds on me, it was more than just dirt that she was washing off. My tough, angry feelings were being scrubbed off of me! The anger was being replaced by love, the fear replaced by hope. Sitting there in the tub with a mother figure like Mattie is to this day one of my greatest memories from my childhood.

It turns out that Mattie looked forward to the weekends just as much as I did. That was when we got to be together. She loved to walk with me around the town and take me shopping for new clothes. So imagine our joy when my father agreed that I could stay with them for the whole summer! It was like a dream come true.

Still, after all that time with her and as close to her as I got, I didn't want to tell her about everything that was going on with me back at Mosher Street. She didn't know the fights I was getting in, the bad accidents I saw at a young age, going to bed hungry, or the lights getting cut off. There was still a lot of darkness inside me that was afraid to let out.

Please, when you find your new mother or your new father, and when they show that they really care about you, let them in! Talking about your darkness is the only way to get it out so that it can be replaced with light. Looking back, I'm sure that if I had opened up to Mattie about what my home life was like, she would have adopted me on the spot! But she basically adopted me in her heart, and the love she showed me at that time of my life was more than enough to set my broken heart on the path to getting fixed.

Like me, I know some of you children have problems you are going through in life. What I want you all to see is that these problems can actually make you grow with all the lessons you'll come to know. Although lots of you little girls and boys are broken, with the help of someone special, you can make things right! And on top of that, you know that you'll always have a friend who is just like you…and that's me: a young boy named David!

Questions to Discuss

1. How did David feel when he realized that his dad left him for no good reason?

2. How did David feel about Mattie?

3. What are some of the things Mattie did for David?

4. What can help you get the darkness out that's inside you?

5. What are some things you have learned from David's stories?

A Young Boy Named David
Book 22
Nightmares From a New Neighborhood

Written By
David M. Smith

A Young Boy Named David Book 22: Nightmares From a New Neighborhood

Written By: David M. Smith

Characters

- David – me
- Mack – my dad
- Jonathan- my older brother
- Mattie
- Willis
- Frank
- The Bay Brothers
- Money

Chapter 1: No Male Guidance

I was getting older and experiencing new things at this time of my life. Being in a new neighborhood with new people around me was giving me new emotions. Mattie and my father were together when I started coming over to visit, and they were very different from the people I knew at 507 Mosher Street. Mattie was the light of my world, the love of my life! She showered love on me like no one had before. In some ways, my father loved me too, but there were other things he loved more, like running after women, drinking bad liquid from those bottles, and working.

As far as him being a role model for me like Mr. Blato had been, my father really wasn't that great. When he wasn't at work, he was running around on the streets. He was basically a grown-up version of my older brother, Jonathan. All I learned from my dad was that life on the streets was wild and adventurous, and that in life you might as well do what you want.

There was no one to tell him that he should stop and spend more time with me. Mattie gave all her attention to me, probably because she knew there was no use trying to change my dad at this point. Believe me when I tell you that street life is NOT as fun as it may seem! Although my dad was doing whatever he wanted, I could tell that he wasn't really happy. He still had a lot of problems, and I hope you don't decide to go that route in your life.

As you might already know, it's hard to get through life without positive male guidance. When you have it, it's good because you can get tips on things to avoid, advice on how to deal with certain situations, and the love and affection that can keep you out of trouble. But when you don't have that guidance, you're just walking around without a clue what to do. That was me. I felt lost and alone. And even though I received heaps and heaps of love from Mattie, a part of me wanted my own father to give me some of that affection.

So it was a very confusing time for me. On the one hand, I would get super excited and run over to Poplar Grove and North Avenue when it was time to go see my dad. I met new friends there like Frank and the Bay Brothers, Mattie would cook for me and shower me with love, and I got to be around my father for the first time in my life. However, he wasn't a father in the sense of caring for me and teaching me how to get through life, so I still felt like something was missing in my life.

Instead, I got a lot of mixed signals from him. One day, he would take me around town with him, introducing me to his friends as "my son." But at other times, in front of those same people, he would use harsh words and say mean things to me, as if he was trying to impress them with his tough attitude. My father was a cement worker, and I found out that his heart was as hard as those concrete blocks he was making. There were times when he would openly say to me that he didn't want me around all the time, and that hurt me deeply, leading to more pain, confusion, and anger.

My brother had been doing the same thing to me. For years, he was the one I looked to in order to be a kind of father figure. But he didn't want to have anything to do with me. He would spend all his time on the streets, hanging out with his own friends and making me feel bad whenever I tried to be around him. We fought each other and screamed at each other whenever we were in the same room, which let me know how much he really didn't like me. This only made me more upset and hurt.

The lack of love and guidance from these males in my life, my brother and my father, set the stage for dangerous times ahead. Even with the love from Mattie, I still needed my own flesh and blood to care about me. Because they didn't, the streets were right there waiting for me, and I ran to it and whatever bad influences were there. Little did I know that dangerous times were up ahead!

Chapter 2: Crimes With the New Kids

This was a rough summer! We were always poor and struggling to keep food in the house. And all around me, people were dealing with their problems by breaking the law. Take my mom, for example. We were tight on money, so she was taking the food stamps from the government and selling them for money, which was against the law. Also, whenever my brother was hungry, he would join his buddies and go to the corner store and eat some food in the back before they got caught. So I was learning from everyone around me that crime was a good way to deal with tough times.

Let me stop right now and let you know that this was wrong! You might have rough times like I did. Money, food, and clothes might be hard to come by. But just because that might be true, that is no excuse to steal and break the law to get what you want! It might seem like the easy way out, but there is only fear and pain waiting at the end of that road. It always pays off to do the right thing and work together to make things better.

But sadly, that's not the choice I made back then. One night, I got word that some of the boys in the neighborhood were going to the nearby

Cloverdale Milk Company to steal some milk and all sorts of juices. And even though I was spending more time in my dad's neighborhood, guess who was there to steer me towards doing something bad? My old buddy Willis!

He had found out about the planned Cloverdale robbery, and he wanted me to be a part of it too. Of course, I said yes. What else was I going to do... hang out with my dad or my brother? Pops was at work, and Jonathan was so annoyed by me that he had stopped hanging out with Willis once he showed any interest in being my friend. They didn't want me, so Willis and the other stealing kids I met were my only friends. I was in with the bad crowd, and I was ready to act out right along with them!

When we got to Monroe Street where Cloverdale was, we saw what seemed like hundreds of company vehicles, all full of goodies for us to steal! To get to where the cars were, we had to climb over a huuuuge ten-foot fence, which scared the lights out of me just looking at it! I was afraid of heights and almost backed out. But when I saw all the other kids climbing over, I didn't want to be left behind. With my dad and my brother rejecting me, I couldn't afford to be kicked out of the only group left for me to join! Also, I happened to be really thirsty that night, so that helped to overcome my fears of going over the fence. But my thirst couldn't have prepared me for the worst!

When I finally found the courage to make it to the other side, I looked back and was a bit surprised to see that Willis hadn't come over with me. He told me that he was going to stay on that side while I tossed bottles of milk and juice over to him. Sounded like an excuse, but hey, I was already over, so I got to robbing those juice and milk bottles. Me and all the kids who had climbed over were doing that for a while, and it seemed like all was going well. Until…WOOP! WOOP!

Oh no! The police had finally shown up, and it was everyone for themselves! Friend, can you believe that Willis ditched me again and left me all by myself against those cops?! That's another reason why you shouldn't go along with the crowd to do bad things. People like that don't make good friends. They care about themselves more than they care about you, and when those scary red and blue lights start flashing, you'll be left hiding under a car, hoping that the police lights or their sniffer dogs don't find you and send you off to jail!

After being abandoned emotionally by my father and brother, and now physically left behind by Willis, my anger was at a very high level. I was seriously tired of Willis being a bad friend. Eventually, I met a kid named Frank and began doing things with him more. He was also older than me, and he was into the same things Willis was into. But I felt better around him because he always made sure to include me in the stealing and selling process. Frank introduced me to the Bay Brothers, some other tough teenage kids from Druid Hills, the next street over. They were ones you didn't mess with, and they added their muscles to Frank's smarts in our group. Together, we were a group of bad kids, stealing from corner stores, selling our "products" on the bus, and fighting other kids who tried to take over our territory.

Because Frank was good at stealing and making money, we were very successful, and soon all the kids on the block wanted to be part of our group. Our bad habits became the new law of the streets. Anyone that challenged us, we beat up. And kids that didn't fit in, we made fun of and picked on.

Sadly, treating kids this way, especially the teasing and bullying part, led to a situation that I will never forget; a situation that many kids are experiencing, even today. This may be one of the most powerful lessons you learn from this young boy named David, so stay tuned… it's coming up next!

Chapter 3: A Moment I Won't Forget

Along with Frank and the Bay Brothers, I was making a lot of new friends on Poplar Grove. I was finally moving on from Willis to hanging around them more, and with all the time I was spending over on my dad's block, we were growing up together. We were going from boys to teenagers, and our violent, bullying ways were sticking with us.

Playing sports, going to pool parties, and hanging out were getting replaced by committing crimes, forming gangs, fighting on the streets, and bullying outcasts. One of the targets for our bullying was a kid that we called Money. To us, he seemed to be a strange boy. We teased him because of the big glasses he had to wear. On top of that, they were cracked, crooked, and held together with tape, which only made us laugh at him more. We said things like, "you're so broke, you can only afford to wear those busted up glasses! We bet your family ain't got no money!" In fact, that's probably why we called him "Money" in the first place… because it didn't look like he had any of it!

Pause!! Major timeout here, kids!! It is never, ever, ok to make fun of someone because they look different than you, or because they might be poor. That's a big no no! After all, was it Money's fault that his eyesight was bad? Was it his fault that someone in our group tripped him and made him fall, damaging his glasses? And was it his fault that his family was tight on cash and couldn't afford to buy him a new pair? No, no, and no! So then, what gave us the right to make fun of him?

Well, nothing gave us the right, and I can't speak for the other kids, but I can tell you why I did it. Remember all that bottled up anger and pain from my relationships with my dad, Jonathan, and Willis? Well, I WRONGLY decided to dump all those feelings onto Money. He was younger and smaller than me, so I wasn't afraid of anything he could do to me.

That's the basic breakdown of a bully: a broken person who tries to break someone else as a way to feel better about themselves. Only, this isn't how you heal yourself. Take it from me. I've been bullied, and I've been the bully. It doesn't work. This is when you need to get a teacher or counselor involved to help you both work on the problems happening on the inside, mainly by talking things out.

The thing was, me and Money weren't in school. We were on the street, *without any guidance*, so there was no one to go to that could help us work things out. Instead, we continued to push Money to the edge by our teasing, until one day he had enough.

We all knew Money's grandfather had a shotgun, because he told us about it every time he had the chance. It was probably his way of saying, "you guys better not mess with me!" But he was all talk, because he never actually went and got it.

Until one day came that I will never forget. Me and Money had gotten into an argument about something, and for whatever reason I decided to hit him right in his face (please don't think that I'm supporting violence... kids, this was very bad for me to do). It turns out this was the straw that broke the camel's back, which means that Money was fed up!! Wow! The words that came out of his mouth at me and the crying and screaming were something else.

After that, he ran into his grandfather's house for a few minutes. In my mind, I pictured him in there crying like a baby after I hit him. But then he came out, with his eyes looking right at me. Also, he was walking toward me in a funny way. I guessed that he wanted to go for round two, so I started walking towards him. We met at the middle of Westwood Street. We were about two feet away from each other, when...

All of sudden, Money pulled his hands from behind him and stuck that shotgun right in my face! HELLLLPPPP!! He was screaming and yelling something at me, but all I could think about was, "wow, I could lose my life right now." Suddenly, nothing was in the world except for me and that gun, and the fear I felt at that moment was off the charts. And there was nothing I could do. If Money decided to pull the trigger, that would be it.

Well, thankfully, he didn't do that. He was just trying to scare me and get back at me. But hey, timeout again!! Because that's also wrong! If a family member owns a gun, you should never use it to get back at someone who has made you upset. That does not help the problem at all. It will only make things worse, and you could end up doing something that you can't take back.

That's it for my story. You can be sure that I never messed with Money again! But there are a lot of kids now who are living in fear of guns. Maybe you see them at home. Maybe you've seen them on the streets. Or maybe... you saw them at school. Maybe a kid who was bullied got fed up and showed up with a gun. Or maybe a stranger with problems that have nothing to do with you entered your school and threatened your life.

Please talk to your parents, teachers, and counselors about gun safety, and what to do when there's an active shooter. You are not meant to be just a young boy or girl. You are supposed to grow up and keep living. Like me, you might be facing dangerous times. There may be hurt feelings, bullies, and guns all around you. But if you take my advice and find a good adult role model, then I promise you will grow up to be the beautiful person you were always meant to be!

With Love,
Your Friend,
A Young Boy Named David

Questions to Discuss

1. How was David hurt by the bad examples of his dad and brother?

2. Was it right for David to bully Money?

3. How do you think David should have dealt with his feelings?

4. Was it right for Money to respond the way that he did?

5. Have you ever been around guns? How did it make you feel?

6. Discuss with a parent, teacher, or counselor what to do if there is an active shooter.